Oxford International Primary

Science

Workbook

2

Deborah Roberts
Terry Hudson

Alan Haigh

Geraldine Shaw

Language consultants:

John McMahon

Liz McMahon

OXFORD

OXFORD
UNIVERSITY PRESS

Great Clarendon Street, Oxford, OX2 6DP, United Kingdom

Oxford University Press is a department of the University of Oxford. It furthers the University's objective of excellence in research, scholarship, and education by publishing worldwide. Oxford is a registered trade mark of Oxford University Press in the UK and in certain other countries.

British Library Cataloguing in Publication Data

Data available

ISBN 978-1-382006613

9 10 8

Paper used in the production of this book is a natural, recyclable product made from wood grown in sustainable forests. The manufacturing process conforms to the environmental regulations of the country of origin.

Printed in China by Golden Cup

Acknowledgements

The publisher and authors would like to thank the following for permission to use photographs and other copyright material:

Cover: Artwork by Blindsalida. Photos: **p18:** Joe Ng/Alamy Stock Photo; **p29:** © Sergio Parisi/Moment/Getty Images; **p41:** Gavran333/Shutterstock; **p53:** Patrick Poendl/Shutterstock; **p54a:** Jiang Hongyan/Shutterstock; **p54b:** Allinone/Shutterstock; **p54c:** G_tech/Shutterstock; **p54d:** SABIDA/Alamy Stock Photo; **p58:** Eliyahu Yosef Parypa/Shutterstock; **p67a:** Evgeny Karandaev/Shutterstock; **p67b:** RTimages/Shutterstock; **p67c:** Ingram Publishing/OUP; **p67d:** Todd Taulman/Shutterstock; **p67e:** Git/Shutterstock; **p67f:** Siraphat/Shutterstock; **p78:** ARENA Creative/Shutterstock; **p86:** Mint Images RF/Getty Images; **p101:** Realimage/Alamy Stock Photo; **p103(m):** Dionisvera/Shutterstock; **p103(b):** Ingram Publishing/Alamy Stock Photo.

Artwork by Six Red Marbles and Q2A Media Services Pvt. Ltd.

Every effort has been made to contact copyright holders of material reproduced in this book. Any omissions will be rectified in subsequent printings if notice is given to the publisher.

Contents

How to Use this Book

The Workbook for *Oxford International Primary Science* supports the Student Book that children are using in their science lessons for this year.

The Student Book includes some pair, group and whole-class activities, hands-on tasks and write-in tasks to test students' understanding and help them learn. It is important to extend these tasks. This Workbook enables students to build on what they have learned in the Student Book to develop a secure understanding of scientific concepts.

Encouraging students to think about and apply their growing skills and knowledge helps them consolidate their understanding and work scientifically. This helps with confidence. Students also have opportunities to see that science is relevant all around them – both inside and outside the classroom.

Students may find it useful to complete an investigation planning form. This sets out all the stages of the investigation. A proforma is provided in the Teacher's Guide. Find out more at:

www.oxfordprimary.com/international-science

Structure of the book

This Workbook is divided into five units plus a Support for Teachers and Parents section and a Quiz:

Support for Teachers and Parents

Unit 1 Living and Growing

Unit 2 Growing Plants

Unit 3 Habitats and Food Chains

Unit 4 Uses of Materials

Unit 5 Day and Night

Quiz Yourself

What you will find in each unit

There are four types of lessons:

Key words and introduction lessons encourage students to read, spell and use the scientific vocabulary in the unit.

Activities build on the work in the Student Book. These help with developing language skills, developing scientific enquiry skills, applying mathematical knowledge and securing understanding rather than just recall. The Support for Teachers and Parents notes on pages 6–11 give you advice on how to help students with each activity.

What I have learned encourages students to talk about what they have learned, reflect on what went well and revisit any areas they need to check. This encourages a growth mindset.

Investigate like a scientist enables students to apply what they have learned in practical contexts.

What you will find in the lessons

Icons show the nature of each task:

Discuss: Students are encouraged to discuss and communicate scientific ideas and approaches. They can work in pairs or small groups for discussion tasks.

Investigate: Students are encouraged to plan, ask questions and record results for each investigation. They are asked to observe closely, make predictions and compare their results with others. Sometimes you will use different equipment, which is available in school. You may also ask students to carry out a test in a different way, to make sure they are safe.

Language support: This icon highlights activities that provide language support through writing frames or word banks. Students are encouraged to write, read and record short answers.

Hints and tips: Students are encouraged to think about tips to make investigations safer or more effective.

Stretch zone: Students are encouraged to extend their understanding.

Mindful moments: Students are encouraged to think about and reflect on what they have learned. This supports students' well-being.

What went well: Students are encouraged to talk about what went well in each module to secure their understanding.

Student Book

Throughout the Workbook, you will find links to the Student Book. Students can refer to information in the Student Book to help them complete activities.

Teacher's Guide

The Teacher's Guide that accompanies this book provides lesson notes and answers for each page.

Support for Teachers and Parents

1 Living and Growing

What students will learn

This unit helps students to understand more about animals and plants, and what they need to stay healthy. They will also study how people stay healthy by eating a balanced diet, exercising and following hygiene rules. Students will:

- find out that animals need water, food and air
- find out that animals and plants are living things
- explore things that have never been alive
- name different animals and plants and where they live
- find out why we need a healthy diet
- explore why exercise is important
- learn about good hygiene
- discuss that babies grow into adults
- give examples of some animals and their offspring.

Key words

adult, diet, exercise, grow, hygiene, movement, offspring, parent, teenager, toddler

Scientific enquiry skills

This unit helps students to develop and practise the following scientific enquiry skills.

Scientific enquiry skill	Page
Ask questions	14, 20, 24
Use equipment	19
Observe	15
Measure	15, 19
Compare	19, 25
Notice patterns	15, 18, 25
Record	16, 19, 20, 22
Carry out tests	19, 20, 23
Group/classify	14, 16, 17, 22
Use secondary sources	12, 22
Communicate findings	13, 18, 21

Ways to help

- Encourage students to use key words when they discuss their work.
- Set out a range of objects that have never been alive so students can handle them.
- Ask students questions about the animals and plants they see locally.
- Ask students to think about what they eat and why they need to eat it.
- Play games by asking students to suggest healthy meals and unhealthy meals.
- Display hygiene rules and reminders in the classroom.
- Display pictures of different adult animals and their offspring.

Helping with activities

The following guidance gives you advice on how to help students with each activity.

Which foods do animals eat?
Explain that students will have to use some of the foods more than once.

Finding fruits and vegetables
Make a large class version of the results so that students can share and compare their findings.

Healthy eating
Help students to produce circles to represent plates. You could allow them to write down their healthy breakfast on a paper plate and display it.

Match the words
Discuss each word with students. Encourage them to say each word out loud.

Exercise and energy
Remind students of the link between moving a lot and using up a lot of energy.

Heart rates
Take special care to make sure that students practise taking a pulse, and help with the timing.

Hand-washing investigation
Remind students to wash their hands for 20 seconds each time to make the test fair.

Hygiene poster
Obtain some health leaflets and posters from local health centres to display. This will give students some ideas.

Your family timeline
Place pen marks or put tape on the pieces of string to help students to split it into the correct divisions.

Measuring heights
Demonstrate the height measuring technique to point out the need for the ruler to be horizontal.

Reproduction
Point out that the words can be written across the page or downwards.

How tall are animals?

Remind students to draw the bar for each animal up to the height on the y-axis.

2 Growing Plants

What students will learn

This unit helps students to understand more about how plants grow and develop. Students will:

- explore how seeds and bulbs grow into flowering plants
- discover that plants need light, water and the right temperature to grow.

Key words

bulb, germination, grow, light, plant, seed, temperature, water

Scientific enquiry skills

This unit helps students to develop and practise the following scientific enquiry skills.

Scientific enquiry skill	Page
Ask questions	29, 36, 37, 38, 40
Use equipment	31, 32, 41
Observe	28, 29, 32, 33, 38, 39
Measure	30, 31, 32
Compare	32, 34, 37, 38
Notice patterns	32, 35, 37, 38
Record	31, 34, 38, 39
Carry out tests	30, 31, 37, 38, 39
Group/classify	34, 36
Use secondary sources	33
Communicate findings	32, 35

Ways to help

- Display the key words.
- Obtain a variety of seed packets and display these.
- Encourage students to grow plants from seeds.
- Help students to find pictures of different plants and fruits showing seeds.
- Explain that plants need light to help them make food. Animals cannot do this.
- Show examples of bulbs and let students plant some.

- Let students work outside to observe plants and where they grow.
- Encourage students to predict what happens if plants cannot have light or water.
- Allow students to talk to each other as much as possible to share ideas.

Helping with activities

The following guidance gives you advice on how to help students with each activity.

Measuring plants

Allow students practice measuring different objects as well as the plant and lines.

Investigating sunflowers

Point out that there will be some variation in the rate of germination and growth of the sunflowers. This is why scientists use averages.

Investigating different seeds

Have a large class results table at the front so that students can share and compare their findings.

Why flowering plants spread seeds

Make an example of the helicopter seed model to hand around the class so students can see how it is cut and folded.

Recording measurements

Explain that small objects are measured in centimetres or even millimetres and large objects in metres or even kilometres.

How a seed changes into a small plant

Point out that students should compare their seeds with the pictures showing the stages of germination.

Which parts of the plant are eaten?

Display some fruits and vegetables so students can look at some examples of plants we eat as food.

Survey of plants used for food

Select a local market or large shop and visit or write to obtain permission for your visit with students.

Do plants need light to grow?

Remind students that only one variable (light) should be changed and everything else should be kept the same.

Recording results

Explain that students should colour in the plant pictures so they represent what their plants looked like in the investigation.

Water the plants

You can support some students by reminding them that plants without water will wilt.

Making an animal with plant hair

Encourage students not to copy the example in the picture – they should design their own.

3 Habitats and Food Chains

What students will learn

This unit helps students to understand more about where animals and plants live and what these habitats provide for these living things. Students will:

- discover living and non-living things
- explore different animals and plants and where they live
- identify different habitats
- explore how animals get their food from plants and other animals
- understand ways to care for the environment.

Key words

adapted, environment, food chain, habitat, living, micro-habitat, minibeasts, non-living, pollution

Scientific enquiry skills

This unit helps students to develop and practise the following scientific enquiry skills.

Scientific enquiry skill	Page
Ask questions	52, 55, 59
Use equipment	44, 49, 50, 52, 58, 61
Observe	45, 47, 49, 50, 51, 52, 54, 59, 60
Measure	52, 55, 59, 60
Compare	50, 51, 52, 54, 56
Notice patterns	48, 52, 53, 56, 59, 60
Record	44, 48, 51, 55, 56, 57, 59, 60
Carry out tests	48, 52, 55, 57, 59
Group/classify	47, 50, 51, 54, 56, 60
Use secondary sources	55, 58, 61
Communicate findings	46, 57, 58, 59, 60

Ways to help

- Read out all of the keys words and ask students to say which ones they have heard of before.
- Collect photographs of different habitats to act as examples.
- Download examples of food chains that contain pictures of living things.

- Take students outside to explore some local habitats.
- Set up some micro-habitats with students – such as bug hotels.
- Display pictures of habitats that have been damaged, to stimulate discussion.
- Obtain and display information about local conservation groups and their work.

Helping with activities

The following guidance gives you advice on how to help students with each activity.

What can living things do?

Create some space in the room so that students have room to act out the life processes.

Grouping

Pre-plan your route around the school so students can observe many living, non-living and once-living things.

Small creature investigation

Point out that the small animals show some variation in their responses and that is why scientists will repeat investigations and work out averages.

Odd one out

Allow students access to books or the internet to research their favourite wild animal as a stretch zone activity.

Plant and animal groups

Ask students to suggest some differences between plants and animals, and make a class list before they start their survey.

Different environments

Stress that plants can be found in the sea as well as on land, and give the examples of sea grass or seaweed.

Which habitats do minibeasts prefer?

If students are collecting minibeasts, insist they use a plastic spoon and wash their hands immediately afterwards.

Different habitats

Explain that students should annotate the picture with arrows and labels. Discuss one example first.

How do animals adapt to their habitats?

Encourage students to compare the length of the animals' legs and necks. How is each animal adapted to its habitat?

Some animal adaptations

Remind students not to touch any minibeast and to make sure they do not damage any habitats. They should carefully return any minibeast to its habitat.

Making food chains

Remind students that all food chains start with a plant (producer).

Humans in food chains
Remind students that if a human only eats plants they are herbivores or vegetarians. Carnivores will eat meat – which includes fish and seafood.

Natural and human damage
Explain that once students have decided whether an example of damage is the result of a natural or human cause, then they link that to the correct heading.

Investigating deforestation
Point out that setting up the sand tray is much easier if the sand is damp rather than dry.

Litter survey
Ask students to compare their litter survey results and produce a class table. They can then use this to produce bar charts.

Pollution spoils our environment
Provide large sheets of poster paper and plan an area where posters can be displayed. They could form an exhibition that others could be invited to see.

4 Uses of Materials

What students will learn
This unit helps students to understand more about materials and their properties. They will study how materials are changed, including by heating and cooling. Students will:

- find out about the different properties of materials
- explore why different materials are used for different purposes
- discover how the shapes of some materials can be changed by squashing, bending, twisting and/or stretching
- explore and describe the way some everyday materials change when they are heated or cooled
- find out that some materials can dissolve in water
- understand that some materials occur naturally and others are human-made
- sort materials into groups based on their properties.

> #### Key words
> absorbent, hard, human-made, material, natural, properties, soft, waterproof

Scientific enquiry skills
This unit helps students to develop and practise the following scientific enquiry skills.

Scientific enquiry skill	Page
Ask questions	65, 68, 69, 70, 71, 78, 82, 83, 85
Use equipment	68, 70, 71, 72, 78, 79, 82, 84
Observe	64, 67, 68, 70, 71, 76, 77, 78, 79, 80, 81, 82, 83, 84, 86
Measure	68, 70, 71, 72, 77, 79, 84, 85
Compare	64, 68, 70, 73, 76, 77, 78, 79, 83
Notice patterns	66, 68, 70, 71, 72, 73, 75, 77, 78, 80, 84
Record	66, 67, 68, 70, 72, 74, 75, 77, 78, 79, 81, 82, 84, 85, 87
Carry out tests	67, 68, 70, 71, 72, 76, 77, 78, 79, 80, 81, 82, 83, 85
Group/classify	66, 67, 69, 70, 73, 74, 75, 86, 87
Use secondary sources	67, 75
Communicate findings	64, 69, 70, 71, 72, 75, 77, 78, 80, 81, 83, 84

Ways to help
- Display the key words and ask students to read them out.
- Display a range of different materials in the room.
- Identify places to take students around school to see different materials being used.
- Ask students questions about how they have changed the shapes of objects.
- Encourage students to feel a range of different materials.
- Create a feely box so students can touch objects without seeing them.
- Encourage students to link the properties of a material with what it is used for.
- Play games by asking for unsuitable materials for certain jobs; e.g. paper hammers.

Helping with activities
The following guidance gives you advice on how to help students with each activity.

Using properties
Lay out various objects that match the properties (soft, hard, shiny and see-through) so students have a good choice to select from.

Useful properties
Stress the importance of linking the properties of a material to its uses.

Which material for the job?
Point out that objects can be made from different materials, but this can limit their uses – a wooden spoon cannot be heated as much as a metal spoon.

Materials game
Encourage students to think of the silliest examples of a material for an object – this will make it more memorable.

Materials in the school
Encourage students to use their observation skills but also have some materials they can test for hardness, texture and strength and to see if any are waterproof.

Slippery or safe?
Allow students to make their own forcemeters from elastic bands that they can then use to measure the amount of stretch.

Testing insulators
Remind students that the only variable altered should be the independent one – in this case the insulating material.

Using the properties of materials
Encourage students to discuss the properties of each material and the advantages and disadvantages of it being used to make the object.

Making a match
As well as allowing students to write an example of how they use materials at home they can discuss why each material is suitable for the job.

Materials summary
Allow students to look back through the Student Book and their notes to review their understanding to date.

Squashing, bending, twisting and stretching
You can ask students to act out squashing, bending, twisting and stretching an object to help them with these key words.

Stretching materials
Explain that measuring stretch is a before and during task – the length before an object is stretched and the length during the stretching.

Predicting
Remind students that a prediction isn't just a wild guess, but an idea of what will happen based on what they already know.

Heating water
Demonstrate this investigation to show students the steam being produced and the droplets forming due to condensation on the lid.

Baking
Work in a clean area such as a kitchen if students are going to taste the cakes that are made.

Making ice cubes melt more quickly
Try to carry out this activity in a room that has warm, sunny places and cool, darker places such as corners and cupboards in shade.

Freezing water
Place some trays of water in a freezer a few hours before the lesson so you do not have to wait for the students' ones to freeze. You can use these to show the class what will happen, to save time.

Ice-cube challenge
Ask students to think back to their work on insulating material to give them some clues about how they might carry out this task.

Which substances dissolve in water?
Explain that when a substance dissolves it spreads out so much in water that it cannot be seen. It may colour the water, but students will not see the material.

Do dissolved materials disappear?
Make sure students see the dissolving of the salt and the salt appearing again after evaporation, as this addresses a possible misconception that salt 'disappears' when it dissolves.

Materials survey
Remind students that natural materials are made in nature and not by humans. They may be processed – such as by cutting or crushing – but they are the same material.

Sorting materials
Provide some large circular objects for students to draw around so they get neat circles.

5 Day and Night

What students will learn
This unit helps students to understand more about how the rotation of the Earth gives day and night. It also explains why shadows change in length and direction during the day. Students will:

- explore how the Sun appears to move during the day
- show how the spin of the Earth gives day and night
- describe the change in the shape and position of the Moon
- investigate how shadows change.

Key words
dark, day, Earth, light, Moon, night, shadow, Sun

Scientific enquiry skills

Scientific enquiry skill	Page
Ask questions	93, 94, 97
Use equipment	97, 98
Observe	93, 94, 95, 96, 98
Measure	97, 98
Compare	94, 97, 99
Notice patterns	93, 94, 95, 97, 98, 99, 100
Record	94, 95, 97, 98
Carry out tests	96, 98
Group/classify	96, 99
Use secondary sources	99
Communicate findings	93, 96, 98, 100

Ways to help

- Ask students to read out the key words and talk about which they have heard of before.
- Allow students to talk about their own ideas about how day and night are caused.
- Download and display pictures of day and night scenes of the same places.
- Download and display pictures of the phases of the Moon.
- Ask students what they have noticed about shadows.
- Encourage students to investigate the movement of shadows outside.
- Constantly stress that the Sun and Moon only appear to move across the sky.
- Use models with torches and balls to demonstrate the spinning of the Earth and light from the Sun.

Helping with activities

The following guidance gives you advice on how to help students with each activity.

Changes during the day
Point out that early morning and evening can have the same light levels so could be mixed up in the pictures.

The Earth spins
Emphasise that the spinning of the Earth on its axis brings different parts of the Earth into light and shadow during a day.

How the Sun appears to move
Stress that students should not look directly at the Sun and emphasise that the spinning of the Earth makes the Sun appear to move across the window.

Keeping a Moon diary
If the Moon cannot be seen due to the weather, you can ask students to predict the shape of the Moon or use the internet to show them the shape.

Moving shadows
Give each group a different shaped object so students see that shadows always take on the shape of the object.

Exploring shadows
Make sure students can observe and measure their shadow sticks at times that span early in the morning, midday and later in the afternoon if possible.

Movement of the Earth
Carry out this task in a large space, ideally outside so students can move and spin safely.

Modelling night and day
Remind students to fix the different parts of their model together loosely so each part can spin and revolve.

Key words

1 Fill in the crossword by solving the clues below.

Use the word cloud on page 13 of your Student Book to help you.

Clues:

Across

    2 Animals and plants get bigger when they ____.

    4 An animal's young or child.

    5 A person aged between 13 and 19 years.

Down

    1 An activity that requires effort.

    3 The kinds of food that animals and humans consume.

2 Look back at the word cloud on page 13 of your Student Book.

The word 'hygiene' is not in the crossword. Write a crossword clue for this word.

Introduction

Wordsearch

1 Find the key words for this unit hidden in the wordsearch.

The words can be written forwards →, and down ↓.

Draw a circle around each word and cross it off on the list when you find it. One has been done for you.

k	x	l	r	p	k	l	o	e	x	n	s
r	e	p	r	o	d	u	c	e	h	o	z
x	n	f	e	e	d	d	u	l	y	g	u
g	u	o	l	a	n	o	e	k	s	w	l
r	w	w	q	l	q	m	o	v	e	b	q
o	b	l	m	w	p	i	n	a	s	k	g
w	w	a	w	s	m	c	w	i	u	y	q
d	v	g	p	d	l	i	v	i	n	g	r

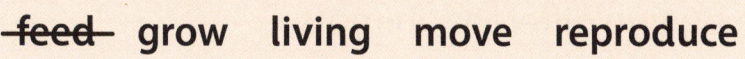

~~feed~~ grow   living   move   reproduce

2 Read out each of the words.

Explain what each word means.

3 Are there any words you don't know? Look up the definitions for these.

Which foods do animals eat?

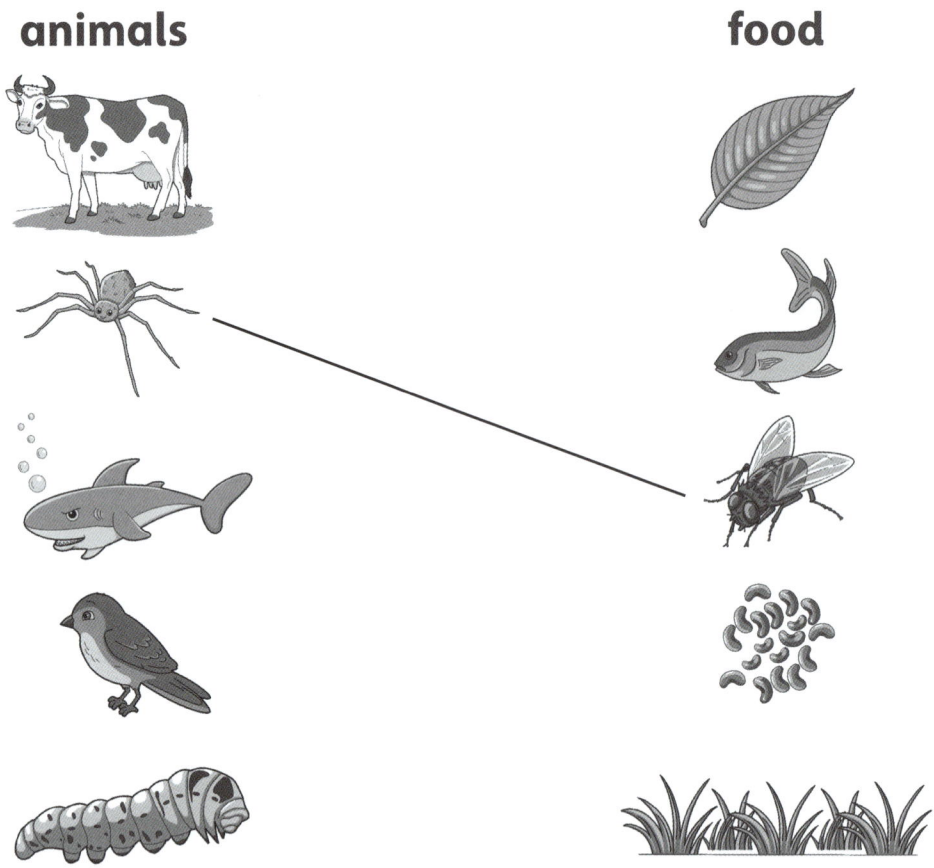

animals   **food**

1 Draw lines to link each animal with the food you think it likes to eat. One has been done for you.

2 Some foods might be eaten by two different animals.

Foods that are eaten by more than one animal are _____
_____.

3 If you added yourself to the list of animals, which food would you eat? Draw it below.

Food survey

This activity supports the investigation on page 15 of your Student Book.

Answer the questions to help you make your survey of foods scientific.

1 How many times will you carry out your survey? _____

2 Imagine you did the survey in January or July. Do you think the results would be the same?

_____

_____

3 How will you record (write) your results?

_____

4 How will you compare your results with other people's results?

_____

5 How will you present your results? Will you use a table or a graph or both?

_____

6 Which of these graphs might be a useful way to show people your results? Tick ✓ your choice.

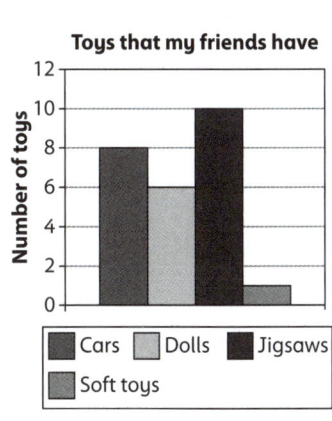

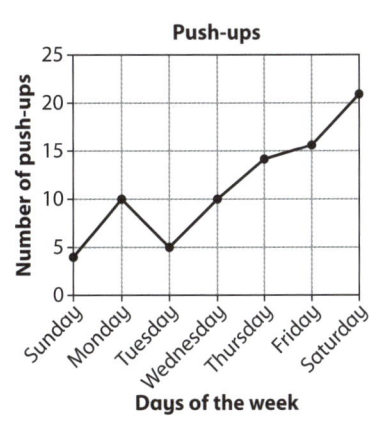

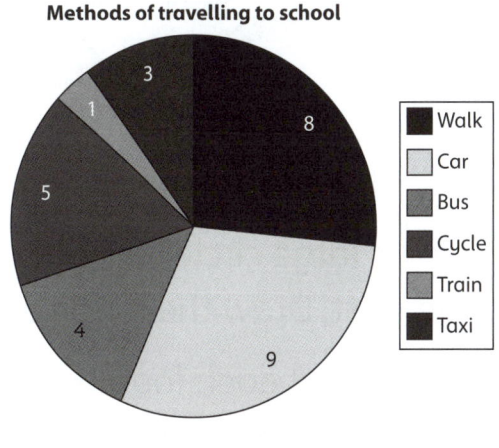

Eating and drinking

Healthy eating

You are going to design a healthy breakfast. Here is a list of foods you can choose from.

apples	cereal	chickpeas	fried potatoes	rice
bananas	cheese	eggs	nuts	tomatoes
bread	chicken	fish	oranges	

 Remember that if we eat the correct amount of foods from each group, we have a balanced diet.

Look at the list of foods and the picture of a balanced food plate.

Draw a large circle for your plate. Choose some foods for a healthy breakfast. Draw the foods or write their names.

Think about each food carefully. Do not just choose your favourite foods. Think about making a healthy, balanced meal.

Match the words

1 Write each word in the box below in the table next to its definition. One has been done for you.

~~diet~~ drink eat food water

2 Draw a picture for each word to help you remember its meaning.

Definition	Word	Drawing
The foods we eat regularly	diet	
We do this when we swallow liquids		
A transparent liquid that does not smell of anything		
This gives us energy		
Put food into the mouth, chew and swallow		

Exercise is important

Exercise and energy

Our food gives us energy. The amount we need depends on our age, lifestyle and the activities we do. We measure energy in kilojoules.

Look at the table. Compare the energy used by each type of exercise.

This cyclist uses up a lot of energy every hour.

Type of activity	Energy used every hour (kilojoules)
dancing	80
gardening	60
working at a desk	15
working on a building site	90
Type of sport	**Energy used every hour (kilojoules)**
rowing a boat	150
cycling in a race	250
playing football	120

1 Which of the activities uses the most energy every hour? _____

2 Why do you think this activity needs so much energy?

_____

3 Which of the sports needs the most energy every hour? _____

4 Why do you think this sport needs so much energy?

_____

5 Think! The cyclist doesn't cycle every day. What will happen if he still eats the same amount of food?

_____

Heart rates

The number of times your heart beats every minute is called your heart rate. You can measure your heart rate using your pulse.

You can feel your pulse where you can feel a large blood vessel through your skin.

Look at the picture. Practise feeling your pulse.

Count your heart beats for 30 seconds. Double this to work out your heart rate for one minute.

How does exercise change your heart rate?

1 Plan an investigation to explore how exercise changes your heart rate.

2 Carry out your investigation. Record your heart rates in the table.

Exercise	Heart rate (heart beats per minute)
resting	
walking slowly for a minute	
walking quickly for a minute	
running for a minute	

3 Explain what happened to your pulse rate during exercise.

_____

4 Why did this happen?

_____

_____

_____

Remember:

- Take your pulse before you start exercising. This is your resting heart rate.

- You must rest after each exercise to let your heart rate recover.

Good hygiene

Hand-washing investigation

 This activity supports the investigation on pages 20–21 of your Student Book.

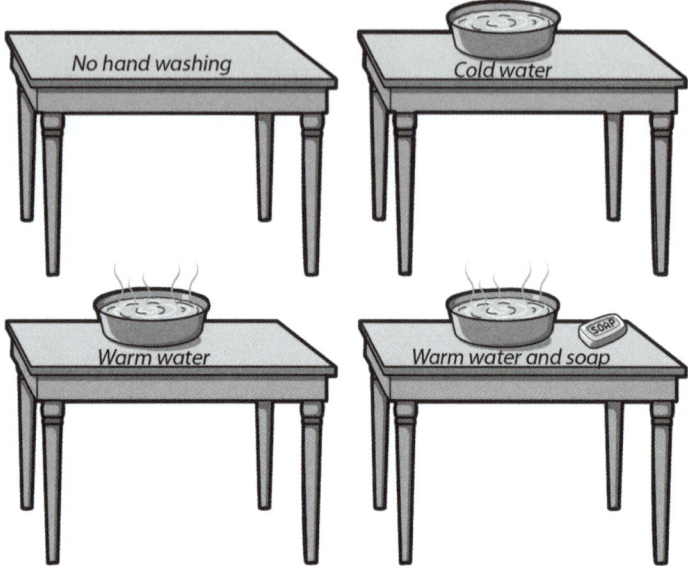

1 Carry out the hand-washing test on pages 20–21 of your Student Book.

2 Record what you see in the table below. Tick ✓ who had sand on their hands.

Type of washing	Who had sand on their hands?			
	Person 1	**Person 2**	**Person 3**	**Person 4**
No hand washing				
Using cold water				
Using warm water				
Using warm water and soap				

3 Draw around your hand on a piece of paper.

4 Colour in the hand to show how clean or dirty your hands were after washing with cold water.

Hygiene poster

Teeth
Brush teeth every morning and night to keep them shining and bright. Visit your dentist regularly.

Hair
Wash your hair often. Keep it neat by styling and brushing.

Hygiene
Bath or shower and change underwear daily. Wash hands after visiting the toilet and before eating.

You will design and make a poster about hygiene.

1 Plan your poster.

- Think about what you want to put in your poster.
- Draw or download pictures. Some examples are shown in the posters above.
- Make the information clear.
- Make sure your poster is eye-catching.

2 Make your poster.

Families

Your family timeline

You are going to make a family timeline.

You will need:
a long piece of string, some pieces of paper and some paperclips.

1 Divide your string into six sections. Each section covers a range of ages.

Section 1: 0–10 years old

Section 2: 11–20 years old

Section 3: 21–30 years old

Section 4: 31–40 years old

Section 5: 41–50 years old

Section 6: over 51 years old

2 Find out the name, age and height of as many of your family and friends as you can. Try to include at least eight people.

3 Write the name, age and height of each person on a separate piece of paper.

4 Use your string to make a timeline. Clip the paper with details of the youngest person at one end of the timeline. Clip the paper with details of the oldest person at the other end. Add the other pieces of paper in order.

5 Look at your timeline. Is there a link between the ages of the people and their heights? Can you see a pattern?

When people get older _____

_____

_____.

Measuring heights

This activity supports the investigation on page 23 of your Student Book.

You are going to measure the heights of different people.

Use the method shown in the picture to make your measurements more accurate.

1 Carry out the measurements.

2 Complete the results table.

Name of person	Height (centimetres)

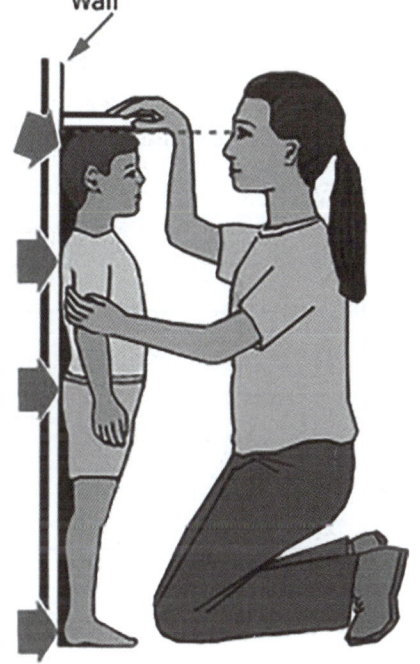

Wall

3 On a separate piece of paper, draw a bar chart to show your results.

4 Who was the tallest in your group? _____

Stretch zone

a Why is it best to measure everyone without his or her shoes?

_____

b Why did the people being measured have to stand straight against a wall?

_____

Growing up

Reproduction

1 Can you find all of these words in the wordsearch? Circle each word in the grid when you find it.

> adult   animal   baby   offspring   parent

d	o	v	s	p	e	c	i	e	a
i	s	p	a	r	e	n	t	c	d
m	e	g	g	s	p	g	a	b	u
o	f	f	s	p	r	i	n	g	l
v	y	p	g	a	a	d	i	l	t
h	r	e	p	r	o	d	m	c	e
q	v	y	t	n	h	a	a	j	t
a	z	b	a	b	y	e	l	p	u

2 When you find each word, explain what you think it means.

3 Write three ways that adult animals care for their babies.

1 _____

2 _____

3 _____

How tall are animals?

You are going to compare the heights of different animals.

Animal	Height (cm)
goat	60
horse	200
rabbit	20
cat	40

1 Use the data in the table to draw a bar chart of the heights of the animals.

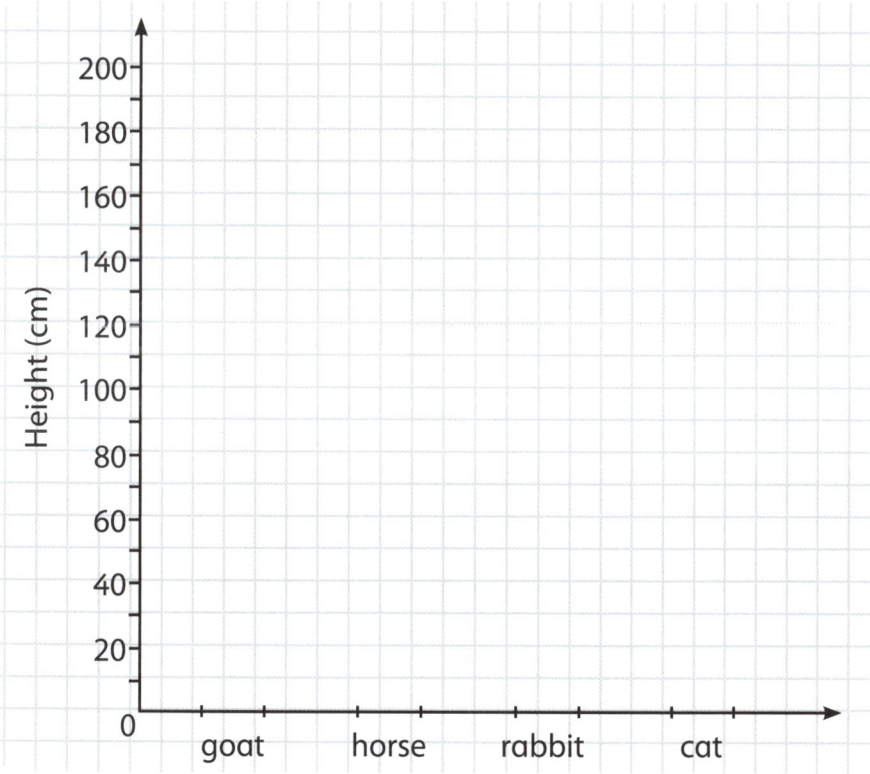

2 Which animal is the tallest? _____

3 Which animal is the shortest? _____

4 Is it easier to compare heights using the table or the bar chart? Can you see any patterns in the data?

_____

What I have learned about living and growing

1 Think about what you have learned.

2 Talk to a friend about something that went well in this unit.

3 Tick ✓ the boxes to rate yourself.

I know that humans and animals have some of the same life processes.	That's easy. ☐ That's challenging. ☐	Pages 12–15
I understand the need for a healthy diet.	That's easy. ☐ That's challenging. ☐	Pages 16–17
I understand that exercise and hygiene are important.	That's easy. ☐ That's challenging. ☐	Pages 18–21
I know that humans and animals produce offspring which grow into adults.	That's easy. ☐ That's challenging. ☐	Pages 22–25

If you want to know more or need to check, go back to the pages in your Student Book.

Investigate like a scientist

Hand washing

Is 20 seconds long enough to clean your hands?

You can test this using a washable ink pen.

Work with a partner.

1 **Draw a design on the back of each other's hand using a pen.**

2 **Wait a few seconds until it dries.**

> Remember how you should wash your hands properly.

3 **Use this to test if 20 seconds is long enough to clean your hands.**

- Did you remove the design?

- Is any of the design left on your hand?

- Is 20 seconds long enough to clean your hands properly?

4 **Now draw a design on the inside of your hand.**

- Can you remove the design in 20 seconds?

You could also use this to test if you clean between your fingers.

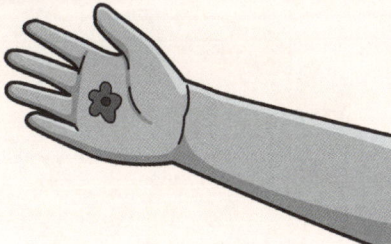

2 Growing Plants

Key words

(bulb) (grow) (light) (plant) (seed) (temperature) (water)

1 Say these words out loud to a partner.

2 Now find any objects in the picture that match these words.

a Circle the objects.

b Tell your partner how many objects you found.

Introduction

Plant words

Look at the following photograph.

1 Find three fruits in the photograph.

Draw a circle around each fruit.

2 Find three vegetables in the photograph.

Draw a square around each vegetable.

3 Draw your favourite fruit.

Growing plants

Measuring plants

 This activity supports the investigation on page 30 of your Student Book.

You are going to practise measuring the length of different lines, using a ruler.

> Always start measuring from zero.

1 Look very carefully at where the end of the plant finishes on the ruler.

How tall is the plant? _____ cm

2 Now use a ruler to measure these lines. Record the measurements in the boxes.

_____ ☐ cm

_____ ☐ cm

_____ ☐ cm

3 Compare your line measurements with other people in your class.

Did you get the same measurements? If not, you must measure again to check.

Investigating sunflowers

This activity supports the investigation on page 31 of your Student Book.

Sunflowers are very tall plants. They have the same main parts as all other flowering plants.

You are going to grow some sunflowers.

You will need:
some sunflower seeds, pots, soil and water.

1 Plant two sunflower seeds in two pots of soil, and water them.

2 What do you predict? Circle your answer.

I think I will see the sunflowers start to grow in …

fewer than two days.   **more than two days.**

3 Check the pots every day. Look to see whether a green or yellow shoot is growing.

How many days was it before the seeds started to grow? _____ days

Was your prediction correct? Circle the answer.   **yes   no**

4 Wait until you have seen seedlings appear. Then measure your plants every day for two weeks. Complete the table.

Seed	Height of plant (centimetres)				
	Day 3	Day 5	Day 7	Day 10	Day 14
1					
2					
3					
4					

5 Did the plants all grow the same amount in the same time?

_____

Plants from seeds and bulbs

Investigating different seeds

Do you think big seeds make big plants?

Work in a group. Your teacher will give your group a seed.

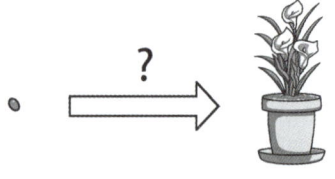

1 Look at your seed. Does it look like the other seeds in the classroom? _____

Is your seed large, medium or small?

_____

2 Plant your seed. Leave it to grow until you see the plant appear.

Measure your plant every day for two weeks. Record your results.

Can you see any patterns?

Number of days	Height of plant (centimetres)	Number of days	Height of plant (centimetres)
day 3		day 9	
day 4		day 10	
day 5		day 11	
day 6		day 12	
day 7		day 13	
day 8		day 14	

3 Compare your results with the rest of your class. Circle your answers to these questions.

a Did the larger seeds grow into larger plants? **yes** **no**

b Was your prediction correct? **yes** **no**

Why flowering plants spread seeds

This activity supports the investigation on page 33 of your Student Book.

These seeds have landed away from the parent plant. They have more light and water.

These seeds may not grow. The parent plant blocks light and takes water.

You will make a model of a seed shaped like a helicopter.

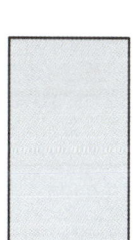 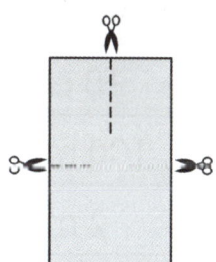 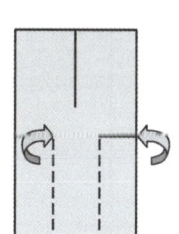 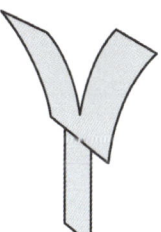

1 Follow the steps in the diagram. Make your model seed and test to see how far it can fly away from you.

Compare your seed with other students' seeds.

2 How can you make the test fair?

3 Record how far each seed spreads.

What was the longest distance?

Hint: Think about the height you drop the model seeds from.

 Stretch zone

How tall can the biggest plant near to where you live grow? See if you can find out.

Measuring plants

Recording measurements

This activity will help you practise recording measurements in a table. It supports the investigation on page 34 of your Student Book.

A scientist has measured the length or height of the objects in the pictures.

| child | car | football pitch | pencil | tree |

The scientist measured the objects very accurately and recorded the measurements in the table.

Name of the object	Length or height (cm or m)
	10 cm
	100 m
	2 m
	20 m
	1 m

Can you help the scientist to complete the table?

1 Look at each measurement and match it to the correct object.

2 Write the names of the objects in the correct places in the table.

Stretch zone

How do you decide whether to use metres or centimetres to measure an object?

How a seed changes into a small plant

This activity supports the investigation on page 35 of your Student Book.

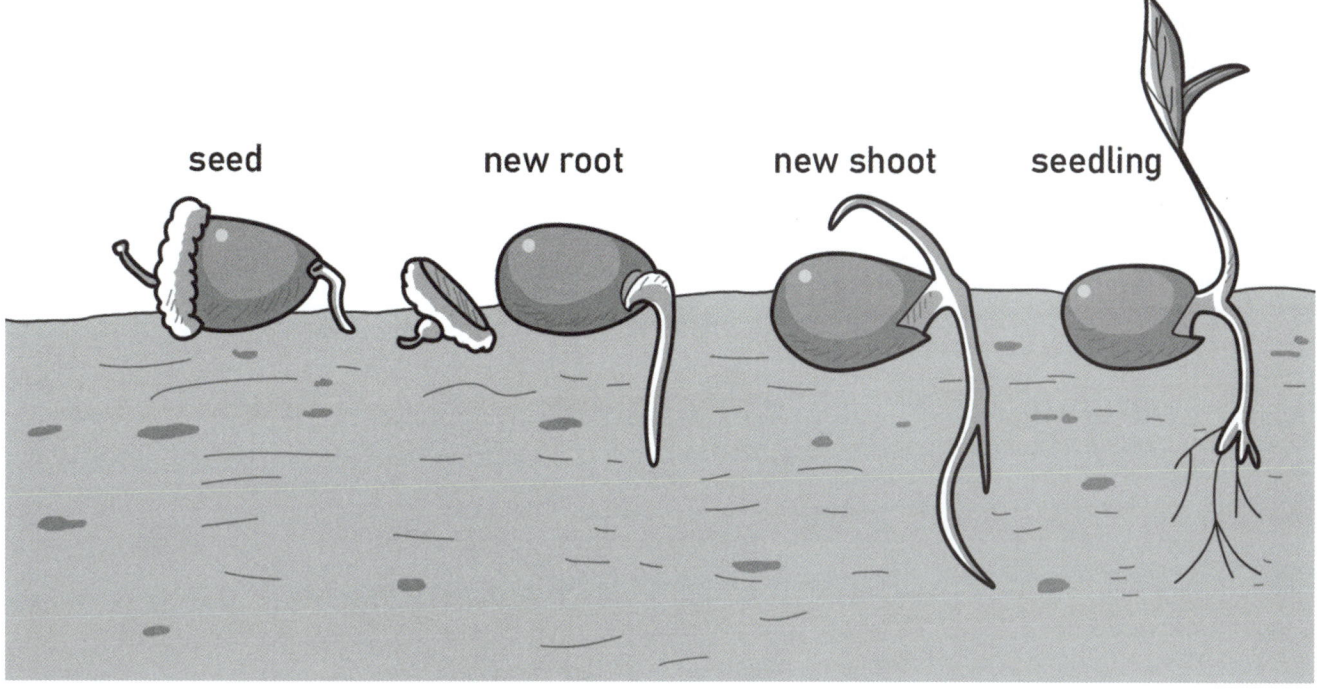

seed   new root   new shoot   seedling

1 Look at the diagram of how a seed changes into a small plant.

   a Which part of the plant shows first? _____

   b Which part of the plant shows next? _____

2 Look at your results from your investigation into growing seeds on page 35 of your Student Book.

3 Draw and label the parts of the plant that grew from your seed.

Fruits and vegetables

Which parts of the plant are eaten?

1 Colour in the parts of the plants that we can eat.

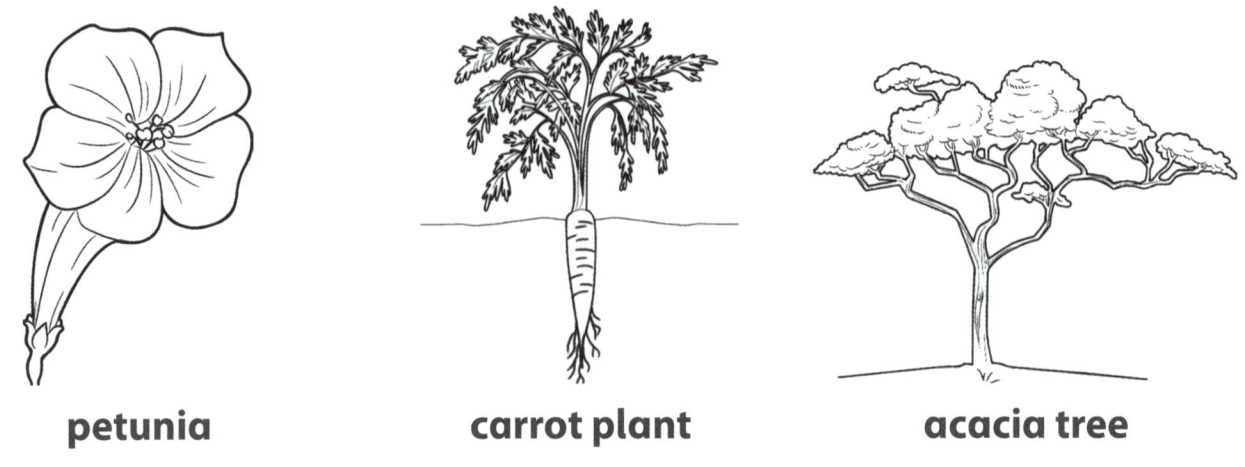

petunia   carrot plant   acacia tree

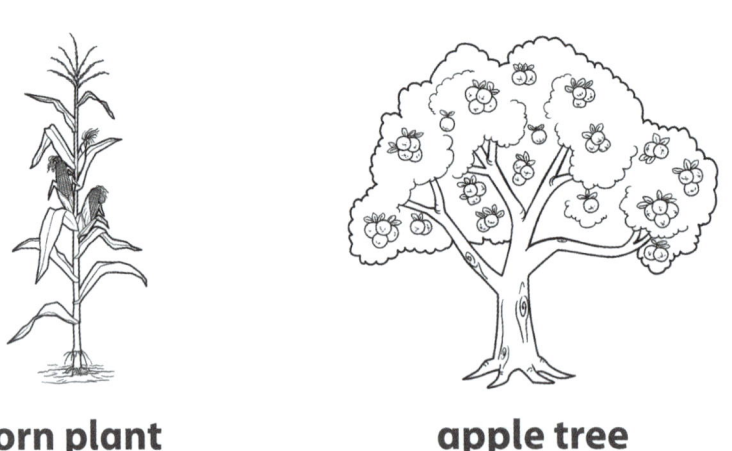

corn plant   apple tree

2 Complete the sentences. Use the words in the box below.

We grow many plants for ___ ___ ___ ___ .

We need to eat fruit and ___v___e___g___e___t___a___b___l___e___s___ to

keep us ___ ___ ___ ___ ___ ___ ___ .

We cannot see plants growing, but we can ___ ___ ___ ___ ___ ___ ___

how much they have grown.

food   healthy   measure   ~~vegetables~~

Survey of plants used for food

This activity supports the investigation on page 37 of your Student Book.

1 Draw your favourite vegetable in the box.

My favourite vegetable

2 You will visit a market or local shop to carry out a survey of plants used for food.

Fill in the table to show the different parts of plants that you saw.

Part of the plant used for food	Examples I saw
leaves	spinach
flowers	
stems	
roots	
seeds	
fruits	

3 Which parts of plants were the most common in the market?

Do plants need light?

Do plants need light to grow?

This activity supports the investigation on pages 38–39 of your Student Book.

1 Answer these questions about light.

a What do you use light for? I use light for _____

_____.

b Where does the light come from? Light comes from _____

_____.

When there is no light, it is dark.

2 You will investigate whether plants need light to grow.

Work with a partner.

a Discuss how you can make your investigation a fair test.

Write your answers to these questions.

How much water should you use? _____

How many seeds will you put in each container? _____

How often will you water your seeds? _____

How long will you leave your seeds? _____

b At the end of your investigation, look at your plants.

Complete the sentences. Circle the correct words.

I found out that the plants in the dark were   **yellow.**   **green.**

I found out that the plants in the light were   **yellow.**   **green.**

I found out that plants need   **dark.**   **light.**

Recording results

This activity supports the investigation on pages 38–39 of your Student Book.

If you have numbers from an investigation to write down, then a table is very useful (look back at page 34 in this Workbook).

When you check to see what something looks like (make an observation) then you can:

- write a description
- take a photograph
- draw a picture.

For your investigation into whether plants need light to grow, you are going to use a picture for your observations.

1 What do your plants grown in the light look like? Colour the picture.

2 What do your plants grown in the dark look like? Colour the picture.

Do plants need water and warmth?

Water the plants

A friend has asked you to water the plants in their garden.

To save water, you must only water the plants that need water the most.

1 How will you know which plants you need to water? In the box, draw a plant that needs water.

2 Complete the sentence. Choose one word from the box.

When plants do not have enough water they _____.

> eat   grow   wilt

3 Predict what will happen if you give a plant too much water.

_____

_____

Stretch zone ➔

Work with a partner to plan how you can find out what will happen if you give a plant too much water.

Write or draw your plan on a piece of paper.

Making an animal with plant hair

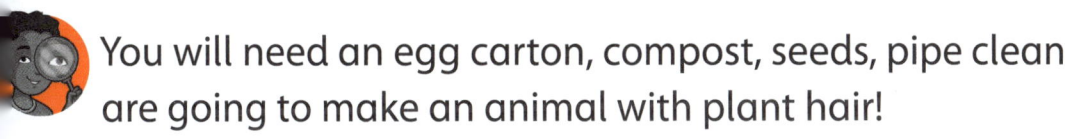You will need an egg carton, compost, seeds, pipe cleaners and straws. You are going to make an animal with plant hair!

1 Design your animal. Use your imagination!

2 Plant your seeds so the animal will grow some hair.

3 Find a good place to leave your animal.

4 What will your seeds need to help them to grow?

The seeds will need _____ and _____.

5 Look at your animal every day and draw what it looks like once its hair has grown.

What I have learned about growing plants

1 Think about what you have learned.

2 Talk to a friend about something that went well in this unit.

3 Tick ✓ the boxes to rate yourself.

I know that seeds grow into flowering plants.	That's easy. ☐ That's challenging. ☐	Pages 30–31
I understand how seeds and bulbs grow into flowering plants.	That's easy. ☐ That's challenging. ☐	Pages 32–37
I know that plants need light to grow.	That's easy. ☐ That's challenging. ☐	Pages 38–39
I know that plants need water and warmth to grow.	That's easy. ☐ That's challenging. ☐	Pages 40–41

If you want to know more or need to check, go back to the pages in your Student Book.

Investigate like a scientist

Do seeds need light to grow?

Your teacher will give you some seeds, clear containers, paper towels, black paper and water.

Work in a small group. You need to plan an investigation to find out if seeds need light to allow them to grow into new plants.

1 **Predict what you think your results will be.**

2 **Plan your investigation. Ask your teacher to check it.**

3 **Carry out your investigation.**

4 **Record your results.**

5 **Was your prediction correct? Share your findings and ideas with the class.**

Remember: Seeds take time to start to grow into small plants.

Key words

1 Find these key words in the wordsearch.

~~adapted~~   environment   food chain   habitat   pollution

Draw an oval around the words when you find them.

One has been done for you.

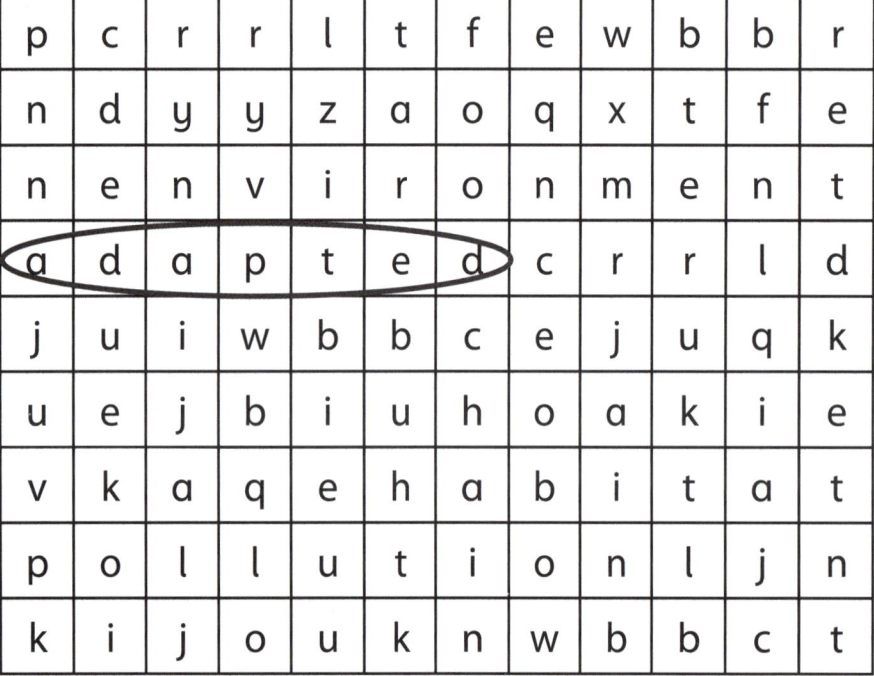

p	c	r	r	l	t	f	e	w	b	b	r
n	d	y	y	z	a	o	q	x	t	f	e
n	e	n	v	i	r	o	n	m	e	n	t
a	d	a	p	t	e	d	c	r	r	l	d
j	u	i	w	b	b	c	e	j	u	q	k
u	e	j	b	i	u	h	o	a	k	i	e
v	k	a	q	e	h	a	b	i	t	a	t
p	o	l	l	u	t	i	o	n	l	j	n
k	i	j	o	u	k	n	w	b	b	c	t

2 Look at the key words on page 45 of your Student Book.

Tell your partner which four words are not in the wordsearch.

Introduction

Alive or not?

1 Look at two of the important words for this topic.

living   non-living

Show the words to a partner. Choose one of the words. Tell your partner what it means.

Ask your partner what the other word means.

2 Look at the picture of the fish tank.

Discuss which things are living and which are non-living.

Write your ideas in this table.

Examples of living things	Examples of non-living things

Once-living things

Sometimes we use objects that are made from things that were once living.

They are not living now.

Wood was once part of a living tree, but a wooden chair is not a living thing.

3 Find three objects made from once-living things. Write a list.

1 _____

2 _____

3 _____

What can living things do?

1 Join the dots to write the words.

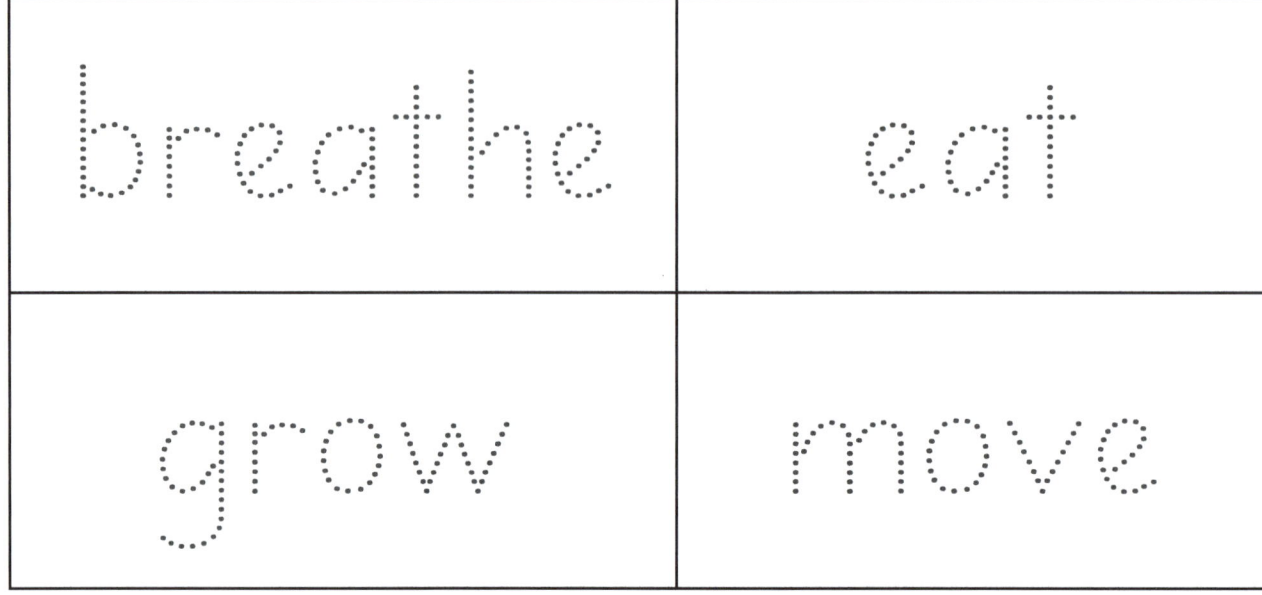

2 Work with a partner. Take it in turns to act out what living things can do. Ask your partner to guess what you are acting.

3 Draw lines to match the words with their meaning.

living things	were living but are not now
non-living things	can breathe, grow, move and eat
once-living things	have never been able to breathe, grow, move and eat

Grouping

You will need:
a large piece of paper.

1 Draw three sorting circles with these labels:

living   non-living   once living

2 Find examples of living, non-living and once-living things around your school or your home. In each circle, draw some of the things you have found.

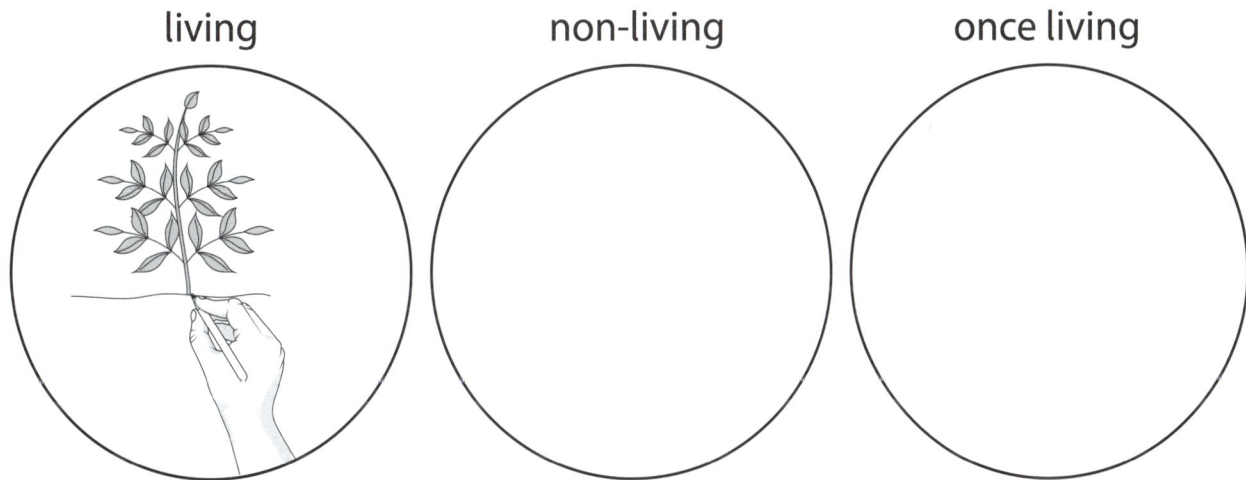

living   non-living   once living

3 Compare your sorting circles with those that other students have drawn.

a Are your circles the same or different?

b Write down one more non-living thing. _____

c Write down one more once-living thing. _____

3 Habitats and Food Chains

Where do animals and plants live?

Small creature investigation

 Where do small creatures like to live?

1 Look at the choice chamber and the small creature.

dry and light

damp and light

dry and dark

damp and dark

> I like damp places and I do not like the light.

2 Guess (predict) where in the choice chamber you will find the creature.

I think the creature will be in the _____

section.

Some students did this investigation. They put 20 of the creatures into the choice chamber for 10 minutes. Then they looked to see where the creatures were. Here are their results.

Section	dry and light	dry and dark	damp and light	damp and dark
Number of creatures	0	2	2	16

3 Was your prediction correct?   **yes**   **no**

 **Stretch zone**

> I like the light but I need water to live.

Predict where this creature will be found in the choice chamber.

I think the creature will be in the

_____ section.

48

Odd one out

Animals and plants need a place to grow, and they need food and water.

Look at the picture. The sea is the home of many animals and plants. In this sea there are some strange animals and plants.

1 Circle the animals and plants that don't belong in the sea.

 **2** Fill in the gaps. Use the words in the box below.

Animals and plants need a place to live and <u>g</u> <u>r</u> <u>o</u> <u>w</u>.

Animals need food, water and a place to <u>s</u> __ __ __ __.

Plants need <u>w</u> __ __ __ __ so they can grow.

Some animals and birds <u>m</u> __ __ __ a place to sleep.

~~grow~~   make   sleep   water

3 Habitats and Food Chains

> **Stretch zone**
>
> Name your favourite wild animal. Find out about where it lives and what it eats. How is it suited to where it lives?

Living in different environments

Plant and animal groups

Work with a partner or group to complete this activity.

Your teacher will take you out to look at different living things.

You will need two pieces of paper.

Plant	Animal

1. Write this word at the top of one piece of paper: **Plant**

2. Write this word at the top of the other piece of paper: **Animal**

3. Look at each living thing carefully. Talk about each one and whether it is a plant or an animal.

4. Write the name of each living thing on the correct piece of paper.

5. Compare your lists with other groups. How are they the same? How are they different?

6. Complete each sentence by writing the number you found.

We found _____ animals.

We found _____ plants.

Stretch zone

Write down the name of one animal and one plant that lives in your area but not in the Arctic.

Different environments

1 Talk about each picture with a partner.

2 Draw a red circle around any animals you can see.

3 Draw a green circle around any plants you can see.

Stretch zone

Write a short story about what would happen if the turtle moved from the coral reef to the mountains.

Comparing habitats

Which habitats do minibeasts prefer?

Work in a small group. You are going to find out whether insects or other small creatures prefer hot, bright homes or cool, dark homes.

What kind of small creatures will you investigate?

Write the name here: _____

1 Make a choice chamber like the one in the picture.

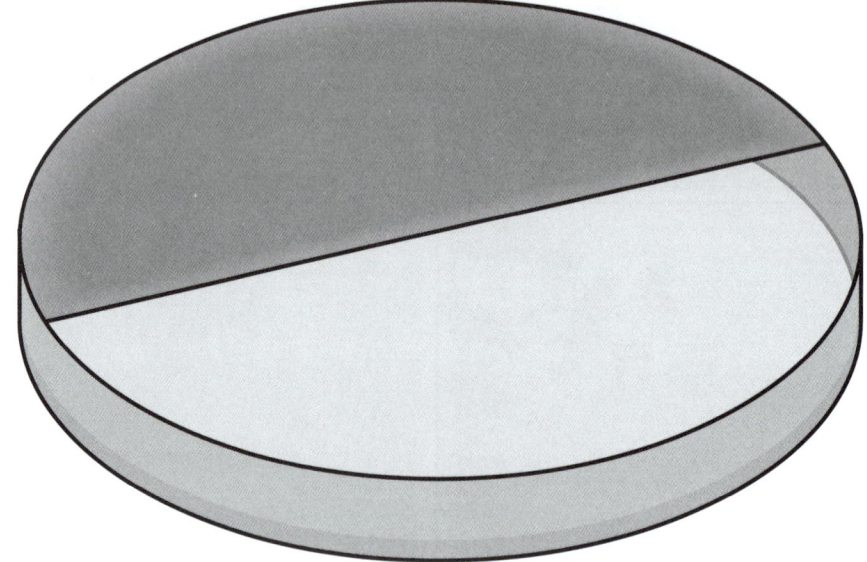

2 Use a light-coloured crayon to draw around the lid on black card.

3 Cut out the circle and fold it in half.

4 Glue the folded card inside the lid. Make sure the card covers half of the lid.

5 Find some creatures outside. Carefully place them in the choice chamber and put the lid on straight away. Do not let the creatures escape.

6 Put the choice chamber in the sunlight or under a lamp.

7 Predict where you think the creatures will go.

8 Observe the creatures to test your prediction.

Where did the creatures go? Circle the section they went to.

They went to the   **dark and cool**   **light and hot**   section.

Different habitats

Use the photograph below to record the different habitats you can see.

Draw a line to each habitat and describe why you think it is different from the others.

Stretch zone

Write out a plan to show how you would find out which habitat in the environment above had the most minibeasts. Include:

- what you will need
- what you will do
- how you will record your results
- how you will present your results.

How do animals adapt to their habitats?

1 Look at the photographs.

2 Which of the animals could eat the leaves from the tree?

_____

3 How is this animal adapted to the habitat?

_____

_____

_____

Some animal adaptations

You have used a pitfall trap to catch some minibeasts.

Now try some other ways that scientists find and study minibeasts.

 Study the methods in the pictures: a pooter, a beat sheet and a sweep net.

1 Choose one of the methods to find and count minibeasts near your minibeast hotel.

2 Carry out your investigation every day for five days.

3 Write down your results in a table.

Method	Day 1	Day 2	Day 3	Day 4	Day 5

4 Compare your results with a group that used the same method.

The results were similar. ☐

The results were very different. ☐

5 Compare your results with a group that used a different method.

The results were similar. ☐

The results were very different. ☐

6 Was one method better than the others?

_____

7 Which method would you prefer to use in minibeast surveys?

beat sheet ☐   pitfall trap ☐

pooter ☐   sweep net ☐

Simple food chains

Making food chains

You will explore how animals get their food from plants and other animals.

Look at the pictures of the plants and animals.

Arrange these living things into two different food chains.

Food chain 1

Food chain 2

Remember to add the arrows. Label the producers, herbivores and carnivores.

Humans in food chains

You will explore how humans get their food from plants and other animals.

1 Survey five people in your class to find out what they have eaten today.

2 Write your results in the table.

Person	Plants they have eaten	Animals they have eaten

3 Are the people herbivores, omnivores or carnivores?

_____

4 Draw one food chain to show how energy has passed down a food chain from a plant to a person in your class.

Damage to habitats

Natural and human damage

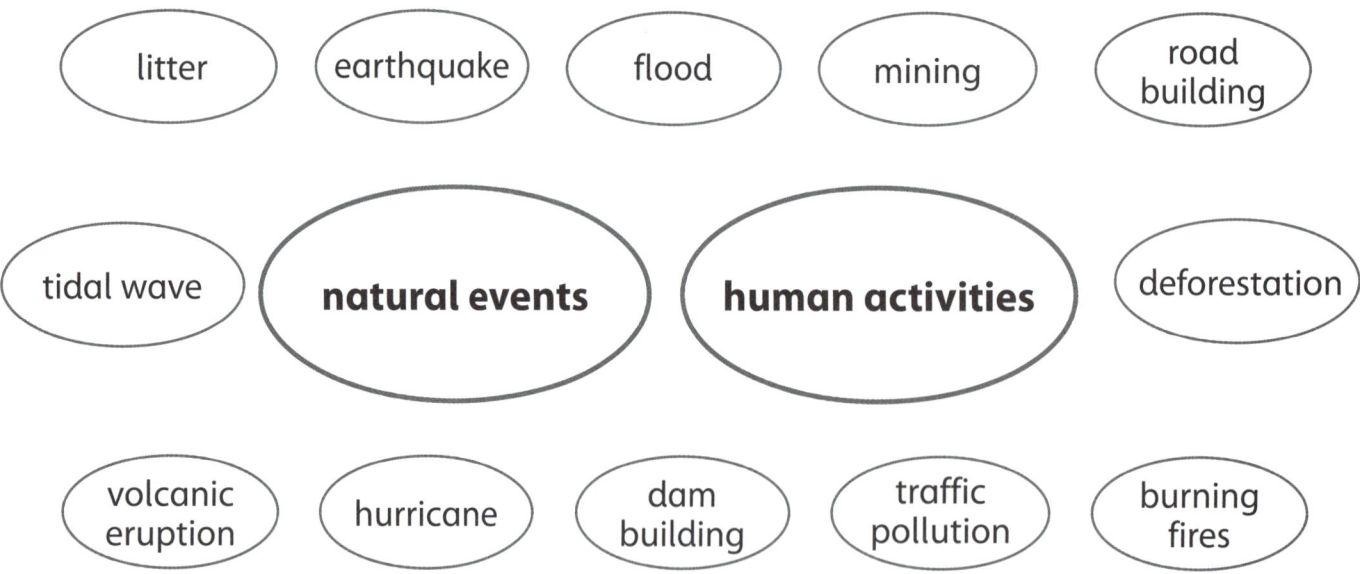

litter earthquake flood mining road building

tidal wave **natural events** **human activities** deforestation

volcanic eruption hurricane dam building traffic pollution burning fires

1 Identify the natural events that cause damage to environments.

Draw a line to link each one to the box labelled 'natural events'.

2 Identify the human activities that cause damage to environments.

Draw a line to link each one to the box labelled 'human activities'.

Investigating deforestation

This activity supports the investigation on page 59 of your Student Book.

You are going to investigate how deforestation causes damage to the environment.

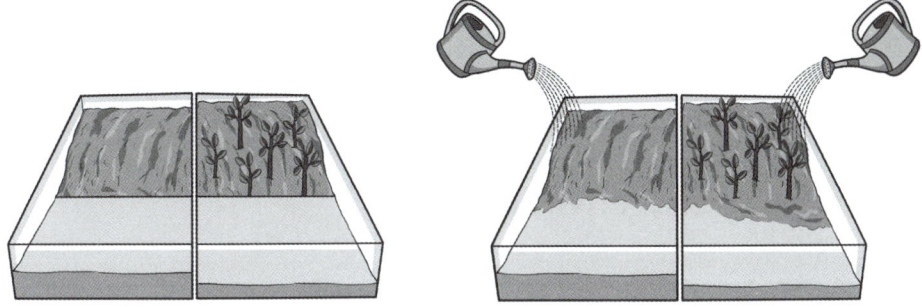

1 Set up two sand trays as shown.

Make the slopes the same in each.

2 Predict what will happen when water runs down both slopes.

I predict that _____

_____.

3 Test your prediction.

What happened was _____

_____.

4 Was your prediction correct? Circle your answer. **yes**   **no**

Stretch zone

Write a short newspaper article to explain why deforestation can cause damage to an environment.

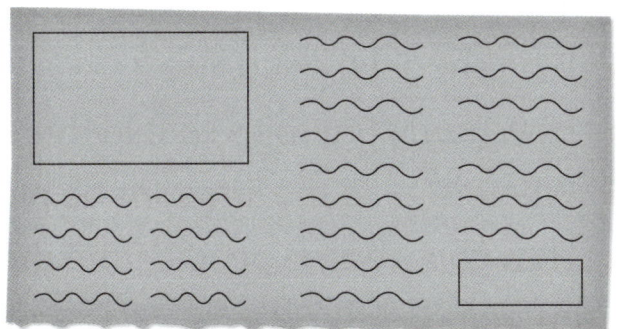

Protecting the environment

Litter survey

 This activity supports the investigation on page 61 of your Student Book.

1 Where in the school and local area do you think there is litter?

_____

2 What are the most common objects that are left as litter?

_____

3 How can the litter damage the local environment?

_____

4 Carry out your litter survey. Write down your findings in this table. Can you see any patterns in your results?

Type of litter	Number of items found
plastic	
paper	
cardboard	
metal	
rubber	
glass	
other	

Stretch zone

Design a survey to ask people about litter. Some questions could be:

- Who should pick up litter?
- How many litterbins should there be at school?
- Where should the litterbins be placed?
- How can we stop people from dropping litter?

Carry out your survey.

Pollution spoils our environment

1 Write the names of some different types of pollution. Fill in the missing letters.

l __ t __ __ r   __ n o i __ __

t r __ f f i __   r __ b __ i __ h

s m __ __ __

2 Make a poster to help people understand how pollution spoils the environment where we live.

Think about these questions.

- Why do people drop litter?

- What should people do with their litter if they cannot find a rubbish bin?

- How can we reduce traffic?

- Where does noise pollution come from?

- How can we reduce noise pollution?

Remember these points:
- Make your poster colourful so that people will look at it.
- Make it big so that everyone can see it.
- Draw pictures so that people do not have to read too much.

3 You need lots of people to see your posters. Discuss with your class the best place to display them.

What I have learned about habitats and food chains

1 Think about what you have learned.

2 Talk to a friend about something that went well in this unit.

3 Tick ✓ the boxes to rate yourself.

I know that animals and plants are living things.	That's easy. ▢ That's challenging. ▢	Pages 46–47
I know that different animals and plants inhabit local environments.	That's easy. ▢ That's challenging. ▢	Pages 48–51
I know the similarities and differences between local environments and how these affect animals and plants.	That's easy. ▢ That's challenging. ▢	Pages 52–55
I know how food chains can be used to represent feeding relationships.	That's easy. ▢ That's challenging. ▢	Pages 56–57
I understand ways to care for the environment.	That's easy. ▢ That's challenging. ▢	Pages 58–61

If you want to know more or need to check, go back to the pages in your Student Book.

Investigate like a scientist

Investigate insect homes

1 Place some leaves on a patch of grass. Place a stone on the leaves to stop them blowing away.

2 Look under the leaves every day for five days.

3 Draw, or take a photograph of, any insects you see.

Warning! Do not touch the insects.

 4 Which insects made a home in the leaves? Why do you think they prefer the leaves to the open grass or nearby soil?

Investigate living and non-living things

1 Make a list of things that living things can do, which non-living things cannot do.

2 Go outside and look around the school.

3 Find five living things and five non-living things.

You haven't moved all day!

4 Draw or take photographs of these.

5 Make a poster to show people what you found.

4 Uses of Materials

Key words

In this unit you will learn about the properties of materials. A property is how a material looks and feels.

Find out about each of the properties below.

For each property, think of an object or a material. Draw a picture for each one.

properties

- soft
- hard
- waterproof
- absorbent

Introduction

Finding different objects

 Look at the photograph on pages 64–65 of your Student Book. Look at all the different objects.

1 Find objects that have the properties listed in the table. For example, you might see a wooden seat. You could write 'wooden seat' next to 'strong'. This is just one of the object's properties.

Property	Example of an object
bouncy	
breaks easily (brittle)	
hard	
heavy	
rough	
see-through	
shiny	
smooth	
soft	
strong	

2 Which properties were the easiest to find?

_____

3 Which properties were the most difficult to find?

_____

4 Compare your table with another student's table. Did you find the same objects?

_____

Using properties

Find and draw an object with each of these properties.

Find and draw an object that is soft.	Find and draw an object that is shiny.
Find and draw an object that is hard.	Find and draw an object that is see-through.

Useful properties

bowl

box

bottle

ball

rug

toy

1 Look at the objects in the photographs.

What materials are the objects made from?

What are the useful properties of the materials for each object?

Record your ideas in the table below.

Object	Material	Useful properties	Not useful properties

2 Look around the room where you are.

Can you find two more objects to add to your table?

3 Look at all of the objects in your table.

Can you list any properties of the materials used that are not useful?

Some materials can be used for a special job

Which material for the job?

Some objects can be made of different materials.

For example, a chair can be made of metal, plastic or wood.

1 Look at the list of objects in the table below.

2 Predict what material these objects would be made from.

Write your predictions in the table.

3 Find the objects around the room.

What materials are the objects made from?

Record your findings in the table.

Object	Material predicted	Material found
bag		
ball		
cup		
plate		
spoon		

4 Did you find any objects made from the materials you predicted? Write them here.

_____

5 Which object was made from the most different kinds of materials?

_____

Materials game

1 Ask someone to be your partner.

- Say the name of an object.

- Ask your partner to say what they think is the best material to make that object from. For example, you say 'bell' and your partner says 'metal'.

- Then ask your partner to say what they think is the worst material to make that object from. For example, they might say 'rubber' or 'glass'.

2 Now change roles. Let your partner choose an object. Try to think of some very useful materials and some useless materials for each object.

Using the properties of materials

Materials in the school

This activity supports the investigation on page 70 of your Student Book.

You can use this worksheet to help you record your results from the survey of materials in school.

1 How will you test the materials for their properties?

Here is a list of some of the properties you might test for.

Write next to each one how you would test for them.

hard: _____

rough: _____

shiny: _____

soft: _____

strong: _____

waterproof: _____

2 Use this table to write down the objects you find and what you predict their properties are. Write the results after you have tested for the properties.

Object	Predicted properties	Properties found after tests

3 Were your predictions correct? Discuss why some of the predictions were incorrect.

Slippery or safe?

Plan and then carry out a test to investigate which floors are slippery and which are not.

How will you test the floors? You can use a homemade forcemeter like the one in the picture.

Look at the forcemeter.

1 What will happen to the length of the elastic band if it is used to pull a heavy weight?

_____

2 What will happen to the length of the elastic band if it is used to pull a light weight?

_____

3 How can you use the forcemeter to measure how slippery a floor is?

_____

_____

4 a In your test, what will you keep the same? _____

  b What will you change? _____

  c How will you record and show your results? _____

5 Carry out your test.

After your investigation

6 Are there any floors in your home that are slippery? _____

7 A cleaner has just washed the floors. Do you think they are more slippery or less slippery?

Circle your answer.   **more slippery**   **less slippery**

Just right for the job

Testing insulators

Which material is best for a warm coat?

1 Set up the equipment shown in the pictures.

| no insulator | paper | cotton | felt |

Predict which material will be the best insulator. _____

2 Add the same volume of warm water to each beaker.

3 As soon as you add the water to each beaker, record its temperature.

4 Check the temperature of the water in each beaker every two minutes.

Remember: a good insulator stops heat from passing through it.

5 Record your results in the table. Can you see any patterns in your results?

Time in minutes	Temperature (°C)			
	no insulator	paper	cotton	felt
0				
2				
4				
6				
8				
10				

6 Which material is best for a warm coat? _____

Using the properties of materials

What do you know about the properties of materials?

1 Talk about these two objects. Which materials are being used? Why are these materials the best for the job each object does?

2 Discuss which words answer the questions. Circle the correct answers. Read the question carefully as some questions have more than one answer.

   a Which material would make a good bicycle?

      ceramic   fabric   glass   metal   paper   stone

   b Which material could you use to make a magnet?

      ceramic   glass   paper   plastic   steel   wood

Sorting materials

Making a match

1 Draw a line to link each material to its properties.

| metal | | hard, strong, shiny, easy to shape |

| fabric | | transparent, breaks easily, waterproof, shiny |

| plastic | | hard, strong, waterproof |

| glass | | soft, bendy, absorbent |

2 Write an example of how you use each material at home. One has been done for you.

metal: _The bath taps are made of metal._

fabric: _____

plastic: _____

glass: _____

Materials summary

1 Complete the table of materials.

Material	Some properties	Examples of what it is used for
metal	hard, strong, shiny, easy to shape	
	transparent, breaks easily, waterproof, shiny	
wood		furniture, spoons, doors
	hard, strong, waterproof	toys, water bottles, cases for hair dryers
	soft, bendy, absorbent	clothes, curtains, towels

2 Compare your answers with other students.

Do you all agree?

Changing the shapes of materials

Squashing, bending, twisting and stretching

 1 Write four words you have learned that change the shape of materials.

_____   _____

_____   _____

 2 Look at the pictures. Use your words to help you write what is happening to the materials.

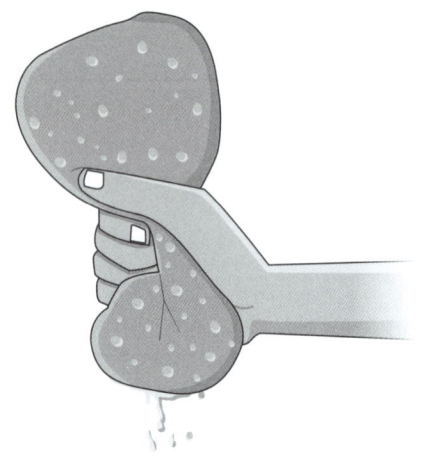

The student is _____ the sponge.

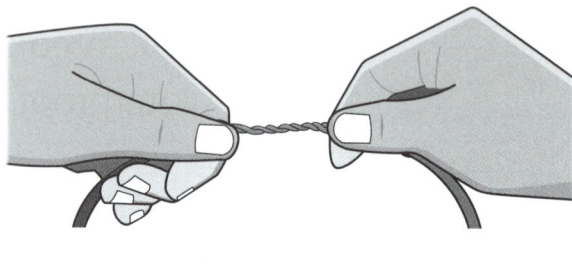

The student is _____ the wires.

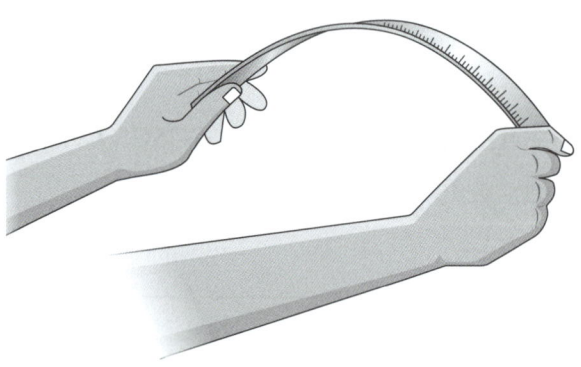

The student is _____ the ruler.

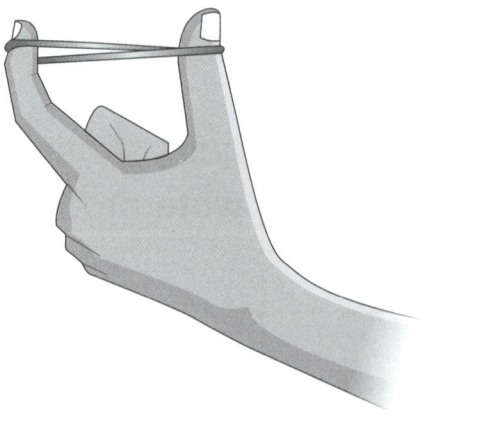

The student is _____ the elastic band.

Warning! Be careful when you are bending and stretching things.

Stretching materials

This activity supports the investigation on page 77 of your Student Book.

You are going to find out which materials stretch the most.

If possible, use the same length of material every time.

You will need:
a selection of materials, a ruler, a holder, a paperclip and weights.

1 Measure the length of each material and write this in the table below.

2 Fix your material to the holder. Add the weights.

3 Measure how long each material is when it is stretched.

4 Write the stretched length in the table.

5 Work out how much each material has stretched. Write this in the final column.

Material	Length when not stretched (cm)	Length when stretched (cm)	How much it stretched (cm)

6 Which material stretched the most? _____

7 Which material stretched the least? _____

8 Can you see any patterns in your results?_____

_____

Predicting

 1 Follow the dots to write the word.

predict

 **2** What happens if you leave an ice cube in the Sun?

Predict what will happen.

The ice cube will _____.

3 Now find out whether your prediction is correct.

- Your teacher will give you an ice cube.

- Place your ice cube in a shallow container. You can use a paper plate.

- Put the container and the ice cube on the windowsill in the Sun.

- Watch it for a few minutes.

What happens to the ice cube?

a The ice cube _____.

b Was your prediction correct?   **yes**   **no**

Heating water

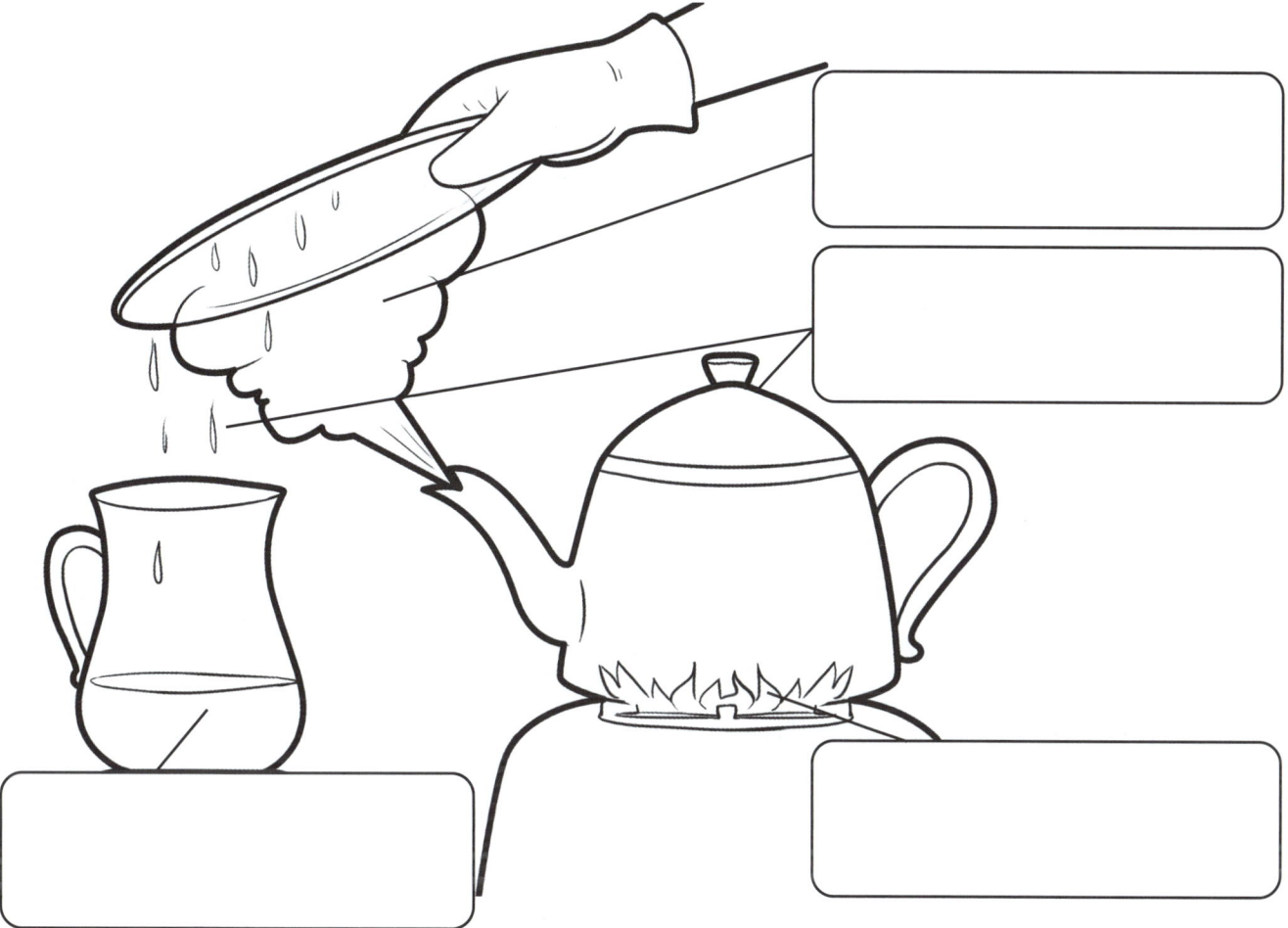

1 Fill in the boxes to label the diagram.

Use words from the box below.

heat   steam   water   water droplets

2 Write your own description of what happens when water is heated and then cooled.

_____

_____

_____

_____

Changing foods by heating them

Baking

 This activity supports the investigation on page 80 of your Student Book.

1 Look at the ingredients below.

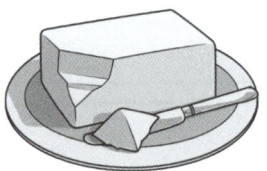    

Predict what will happen if you mix them together and bake them in the oven. Circle what you think will happen:

a The ingredients will become hot.

b The ingredients will change to new materials.

c The materials will stay the same.

Warning! An adult will put your cake mixture in the oven and take out the cakes when they are ready. You must allow them to cool.

2 Why does an adult have to be careful when putting the cakes in and taking them out of the oven?

_____

3 Do the cakes look like any of the ingredients? Circle your answer.

yes   **no**

4 Did heating the ingredients change them? Circle your answer.

yes   **no**

Making ice cubes melt more quickly

This activity supports the investigation on page 81 of your Student Book.

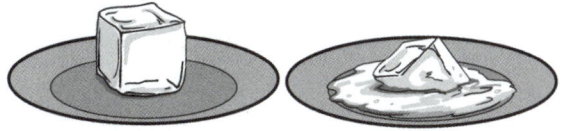

Take your five ice cubes.

You will need: five ice cubes, five small dishes and a timer.

1 Place the ice cubes in different places around the room. Write in the table where each cube was placed.

2 Predict which ice cube will melt first. Put a tick ✓ next to the location in the table.

3 Predict which ice cube will melt last. Put a cross ✗ next to the location in the table.

Where the ice cube was placed	Ice cube I predict will melt first (✓)	Ice cube I predict will melt last (✗)	How long the ice cube took to melt (minutes)

4 Start your timer as soon as you have placed the ice cubes.

How will you know when an ice cube has melted?

_____

5 Write down in the table how long it takes each ice cube to melt.

6 Why did the ice melt at different rates in different places?

Cooling materials

Freezing water

Look at the picture. What will happen to the water in the tray if you put it in the freezer for three or four hours?

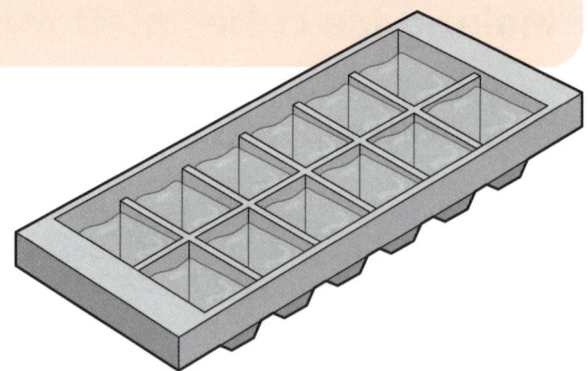

1 Predict what will happen. Write your answer.

_____

2 Place some water in a freezer to test your prediction.

Was your prediction correct? Circle your answer.   **yes**   **no**

What will happen if you now take the tray out of the freezer and leave it in a sunny spot for an hour?

3 Predict what will happen. Draw a picture to show your answer.

4 Place your tray in a sunny spot to test your prediction.

Was your prediction correct? Circle your answer.   **yes**   **no**

5 With a partner, talk about the changes you saw during the cooling and heating of the water.

Ice-cube challenge

 You are going to investigate how long you can keep an ice cube solid.

Imagine the freezer in a cafe is broken.

The ice cubes inside the freezer are melting. They are turning into water.

The cafe owner has asked your science team for help.

1 Plan how you can keep ice cubes solid for as long as possible.

- You can use materials your teacher has given you.
- You can make containers out of the materials.
- You could wrap your ice cubes in the materials.

2 Predict which material and method will keep the ice cubes solid for the longest time.

Write down your prediction.

I predict that _____ will keep the ice cubes solid for the longest.

3 Investigate the different materials and different methods. Record your results.

4 Was your prediction correct? Circle your answer.   **yes**   **no**

 Stretch zone

Write a short letter to the cafe owner to explain your best method.
Include a drawing and your results.

Which substances dissolve in water?

This activity supports the investigation on page 85 of your Student Book.

This activity supports the investigation on page 85 of your Student Book.

You will need: beakers, water, a spoon and materials to test (for example, salt, sugar, sand).

Your teacher will give you some different materials to test if they dissolve in water.

1 Predict whether each material will dissolve. Write your prediction in the table below.

2 Half fill each of your beakers with water.

3 Put one spoonful of each material into a different beaker. Stir the material and the water.

Talk to a partner about why you should stir each jar the same number of times.

4 Did the material dissolve? Write your results in the table. One example has been done for you.

Material	Prediction: Will the material dissolve?	Did the material dissolve?
salt	yes	yes

Do dissolved materials disappear?

You will need:
a beaker, water, salt, a spoon and a small dish.

Do materials disappear when they dissolve? Carry out this investigation to find the answer.

1 Add salt to some water in a beaker.

2 Stir the salt and water.

3 What do you see? What has happened to the salt? Write down your observations.

_____

4 Pour a small amount of the salt and water mixture into a small dish.

5 Leave the dish in a warm place, such as a sunny windowsill.

6 Look at your dish every 30 minutes, for two hours.

Write down what you see in the dish every time.

Time in minutes	What I can see
0	
30	
60	
90	
120	

With a partner, talk about what this investigation tells you about dissolving.

Did the salt disappear when it dissolved?

Circle your answer.   **yes**   **no**

Natural or not natural?

Materials survey

Look at the photograph below and on page 86 of your Student Book.

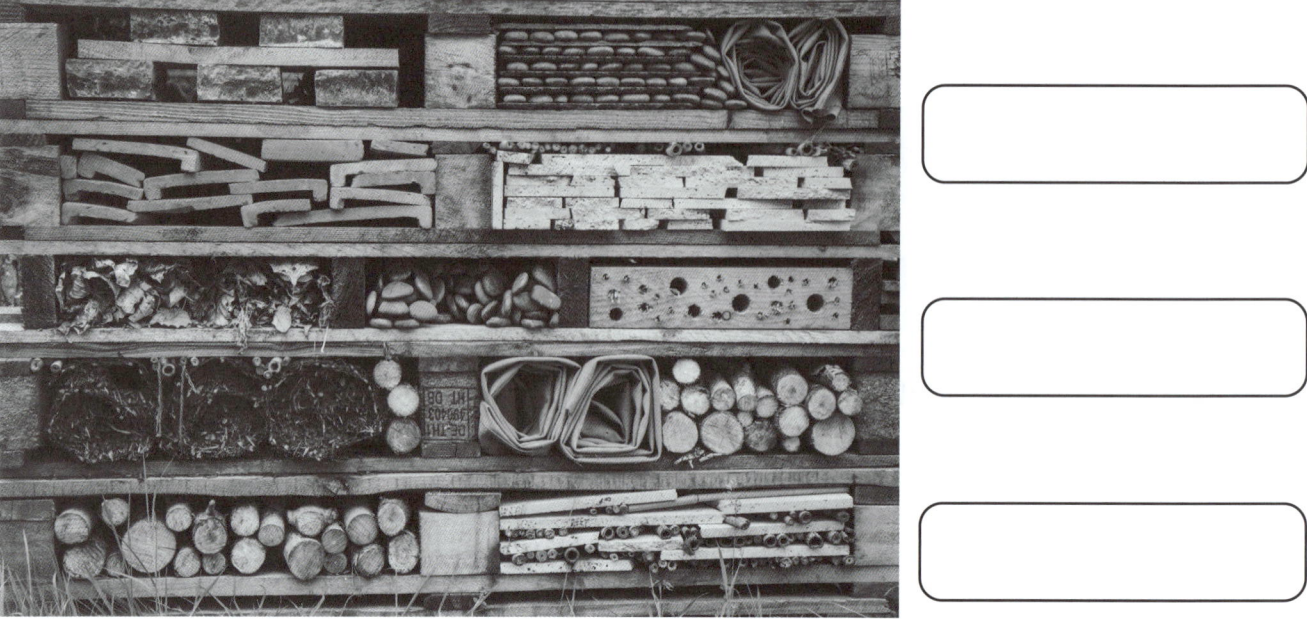

1 Identify three different natural materials you can see in the photograph.

   a Write the names of the materials in the boxes above.

   b Draw a line from each box to the material in the photograph.

2 Look around the room. Identify three objects made from materials that are not natural. You might find plastic, metals, glass or human-made fabrics.

   Draw the three objects.

Sorting materials

This activity supports the investigation on page 87 of your Student Book.

natural   human-made

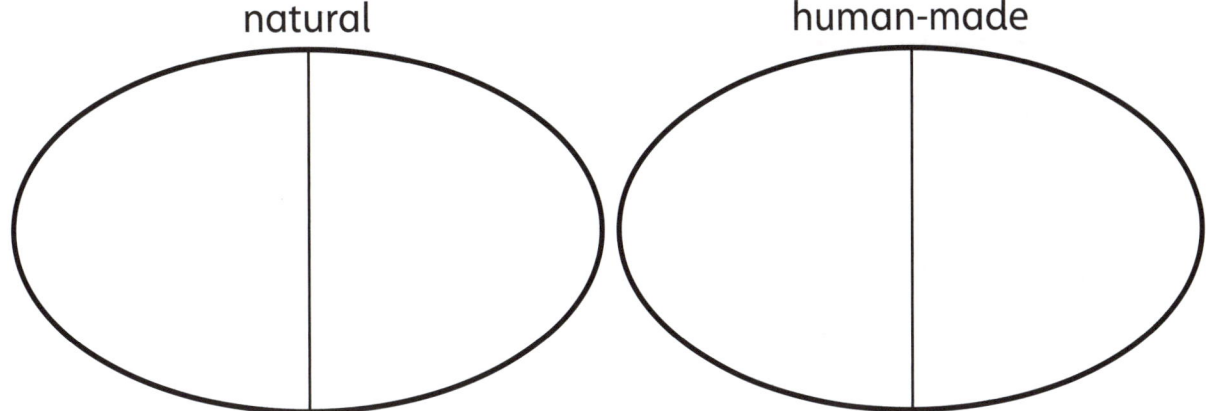

Draw large versions of the sorting circles shown above.

1 Look at the objects you have been given.

2 Sort them into natural materials and materials that are not natural (human-made).

3 Place the objects into the correct sorting circle.

How many objects did you find made of natural materials? Write the number in the sentence.

I found _____ objects made from natural materials.

How many objects did you find made of human-made materials? Write the number in the sentence.

I found _____ objects made of human-made materials.

4 a Look at the human-made materials. Now sort all the plastic objects into a pile.

b Look at the natural materials. Now sort all the wooden objects into a pile.

c Write one difference between the wooden and plastic objects.

What I have learned about uses of materials

1 Think about what you have learned.

2 Talk to a friend about something that went well in this unit.

3 Tick ✓ the boxes to rate yourself.

I know that every material has specific properties.	That's easy. ☐ That's challenging. ☐	Pages 66–71
I know that materials are chosen for specific purposes because of their properties.	That's easy. ☐ That's challenging. ☐	Pages 72–73
I can sort materials according to their properties.	That's easy. ☐ That's challenging. ☐	Pages 74–75
I know how materials can change shape.	That's easy. ☐ That's challenging. ☐	Pages 76–83
I can recognise that some materials can dissolve in water.	That's easy. ☐ That's challenging. ☐	Pages 84–85
I know that some materials occur naturally and others are human-made.	That's easy. ☐ That's challenging. ☐	Pages 86–87

☺ If you want to know more or need to check, go back to the pages in your Student Book.

Investigate like a scientist

Designing and testing a Sun and rain protector

You are going to work with a small group to design one object that will protect you from the Sun and the rain.

1 **Think about the properties that the materials will need for this object. Use your knowledge of materials.**

   Make a list of the materials you will use. Explain why you have chosen them.

2 **Make a model of your object.**

3 **How will you test the materials?**

4 **Would your object protect you from the Sun and the rain?**

5 **What would you like to change to make it better if you could?**

Key words

1 Join the dots to find two key words for this unit.

2 Read out the words.

3 a Think about what you do at these times.

   b Find pictures of things you do.

   c Cut them out and stick them around the words.

Introduction

More key words

1 Join the dots to spell out other key words for this unit.

2 Choose one of the words and draw a picture to show people what the word means.

The Sun appears to move in the sky

Changes during the day

The same place can look so different during a day. Can you think why?

1 Label the pictures to show the time of day. Choose the correct words from box below.

afternoon   midday   morning   night

2 Which two times of the day were easy to mix up?

_____ and _____

 **Stretch zone**

Does it help to know which direction is east? Why?

_____

The Earth spins

Look at the picture of the Earth. Complete the sentences.

Use the words in the box below.

The part of the Earth labelled A is in _____. We call

this _____.

The part of the Earth labelled B is in _____. We call

this _____.

> darkness   day   night   sunlight

Stretch zone

Answer the questions below.

a How long will it take for part B of the Earth to be in bright sunlight?

_____

b How long will it take for part A of the Earth to be in total darkness?

_____

c How long will it take for part A to move all the way round and back
to where it is now?

_____

Tracking the Sun and Moon in the sky

How the Sun appears to move

 You are going to track how the Sun appears to move in the sky.

Your teacher will give you some stickers.

1 Stand a few metres away from a window.

2 Ask a partner to stand near the window with some stickers. Help your partner to put a sticker on the window so it covers the Sun.

3 Do this four times during the day.

4 Draw the shape you predict the stickers will make.

 **Warning!**
Never look directly at the Sun because this can damage your eyes.

5 Have your stickers moved across the window? Circle your answer.

yes   **no**

6 Explain why some people think that the Sun moves across the sky.

_____

_____

_____

Keeping a Moon diary

You are going to keep a diary of the phases of the Moon.

1 Draw the shape of the Moon every night for a month.

2 Use the grid below or you could make a larger version. Use a ruler and sharp pencil. Make each box large enough for you to draw the Moon inside each one.

My Moon diary

○	○	○	○	○	○	○
Day 1	Day 2	Day 3	Day 4	Day 5	Day 6	Day 7
○	○	○	○	○	○	○
Day 8	Day 9	Day 10	Day 11	Day 12	Day 13	Day 14
○	○	○	○	○	○	○
Day 15	Day 16	Day 17	Day 18	Day 19	Day 20	Day 21
○	○	○	○	○	○	○
Day 22	Day 23	Day 24	Day 25	Day 26	Day 27	Day 28
○	○	○				
Day 29	Day 30	Day 31				

3 At the end of the month, label the main phases of the Moon.

Shadows change during the day

Moving shadows

 Work with a partner for this investigation. Your teacher will give you an object and a torch to help you investigate shadows.

1 Place the object on a piece of paper on the table. Make sure the object does not fall over.

2 Shine the torch on the object. Shine it straight at the object so that it forms a good shadow. This is like the Sun shining on the object.

3 Draw around the shadow of the object.

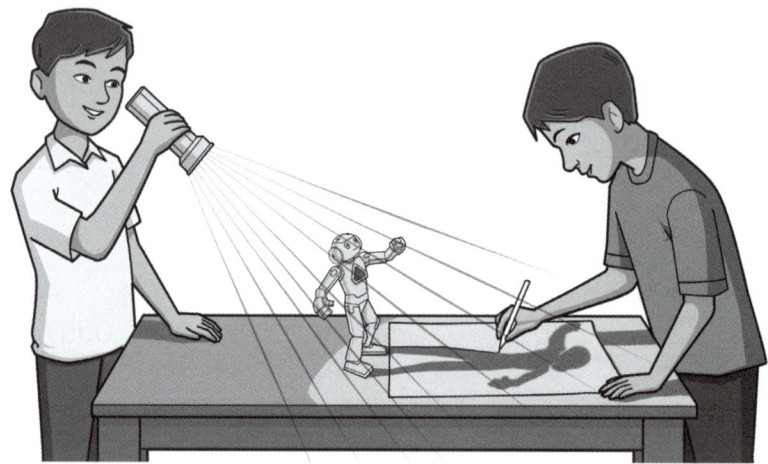

4 Now move the torch to the right-hand side of the object.

5 Draw around the shadow. Compare this shadow with the first one you drew.

6 Move the torch two more times until you have moved all the way around the object. Draw around the shadow each time.

7 Compare all your drawings of the shadows.

Did the shadow move? Circle your answer.   **yes**   **no**

Stretch zone

Investigate what happens when the torch is held higher or lower. Draw the shadows that are made.

Exploring shadows

This activity supports the investigation on page 97 of your Student Book.

1 Set up a shadow stick as shown in the drawing.

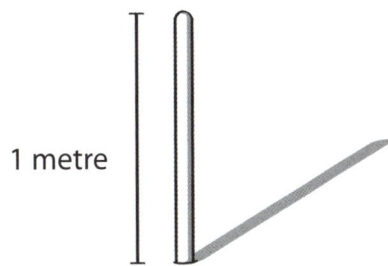

1 metre

2 Measure the direction and length of the shadow at the start of the investigation. Write down your results in the table below. Remember to write down the time of day. Can you see any patterns in your results?

Time	Predicted length of shadow (cm)	Measured length of shadow (cm)	Predicted direction of shadow (north, south, east or west)	Direction of shadow (north, south, east or west)

3 Predict the direction and length of the shadow in one hour, two hours, three hours and four hours. Write your predictions in the table.

4 Measure the shadow every hour to test your predictions. Write down your results in the table.

5 Design a short presentation of your results to tell the class about your investigation.

You could make a poster, write a computer presentation or give a short talk.

The Earth is spinning

Movement of the Earth

You are going to model how the Earth and Moon move around the Sun.

Work in a group of three.

1 One student must hold a source of light very still. They are modelling the Sun.

Complete the sentence. You can use these letters to help you.

| n | o | u | v |

We must hold the light very still because the __S__ __ __ __ does not __m__ __ __ __e__.

2 The other two students will model how the Earth and Moon move.

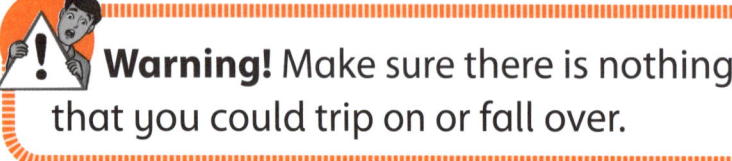

Warning! Make sure there is nothing that you could trip on or fall over.

3 Find a big empty space.

4 One person is the Earth. Remember that the Earth spins on its own axis. Model this by turning around on the spot.

5 The Earth also moves around the Sun. Remember that the Earth spins on its own axis and around the Sun at the same time! The spin on the axis is faster than the movement of the Earth around the Sun.

6 One person is the Moon. Remember that the Moon moves slowly around the Earth as the Earth orbits the Sun.

Modelling night and day

You are going to make a model to show why the Earth has day and night.

You will need: a paper plate, card, coloured pens or pencils, a jar lid, paper fasteners, scissors, glue and black paper.

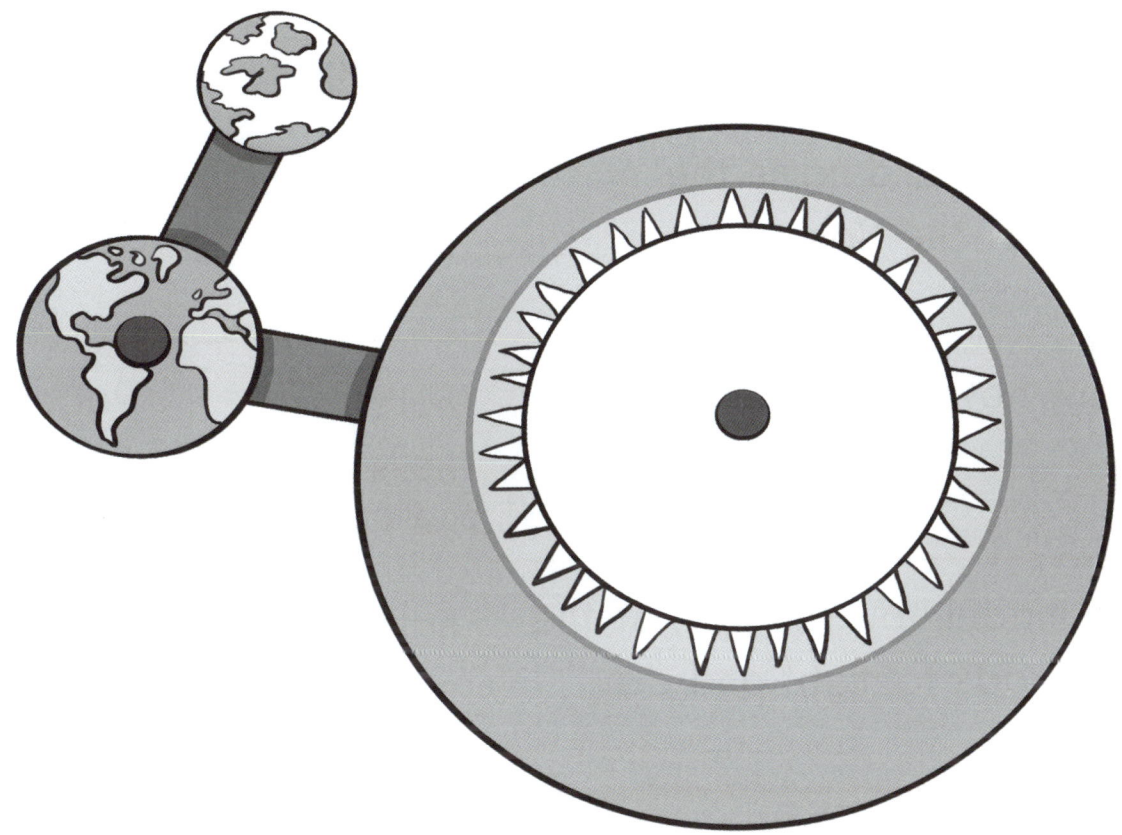

1. Design your model. You can use the picture to give you some clues.

   Make sure the Earth can spin. You can add the Moon if you wish.

   Remember that the Moon will spin around or orbit the Earth.

2. Draw some countries onto your Earth. Use an atlas or the internet to help you.

3. Set up your model and then use black paper to cover the half of the Earth that will be in the dark. It will be night there.

4. Label your model to show the Sun, Earth, Moon, day and night.

5. Demonstrate your model to others in your class.

What I have learned about day and night

1 Think about what you have learned.

2 Talk to a friend about something that went well in this unit.

3 Tick ✓ the boxes to rate yourself.

I know how the Sun appears to move in the sky.	That's easy. ☐ That's challenging. ☐	Pages 92–94
I can draw and name the phases of the Moon.	That's easy. ☐ That's challenging. ☐	Page 95
I know how shadows change.	That's easy. ☐ That's challenging. ☐	Pages 96–97
I can model how the spin of the Earth leads to night and day.	That's easy. ☐ That's challenging. ☐	Pages 98–99

If you want to know more or need to check, go back to the pages in your Student Book.

Investigate like a scientist

Making a sundial

People have been using shadows to tell the time for thousands of years.

Think about how shadows change during the day.

1 Design a sundial using a paper plate and a pencil as the pointer or shadow stick.

2 Set up your sundial in the Sun and record the shadow at 10am, 12pm and 2pm.

3 Draw in some other times. For example, you can predict that 11am will be between 10am and 12pm.

4 The next day, test your sundial by trying to tell the time without a watch or clock.

How accurate was it?

Think of some improvements and then display your sundial for the rest of the class to see.

 Stretch zone ➡

How could you use your sundial to tell when it is 10:30am or 2:30pm?

Quiz Yourself

① Living and Growing

1 a   Follow the maze to find out what the animal is doing. Circle the answer.

b   Complete this sentence.

Living things can breathe, eat, m_____ and grow.

2 Look at the flowchart. It shows some different food choices. Choose three different paths through the flowchart. You can choose one food on each row.

a Choose one healthy food and two less healthy foods. Draw a red line to show this path.

b Choose two healthy foods and one less healthy food. Draw an orange line to show this path.

c Choose three healthy foods. Draw a green line to show this path.

Food choices

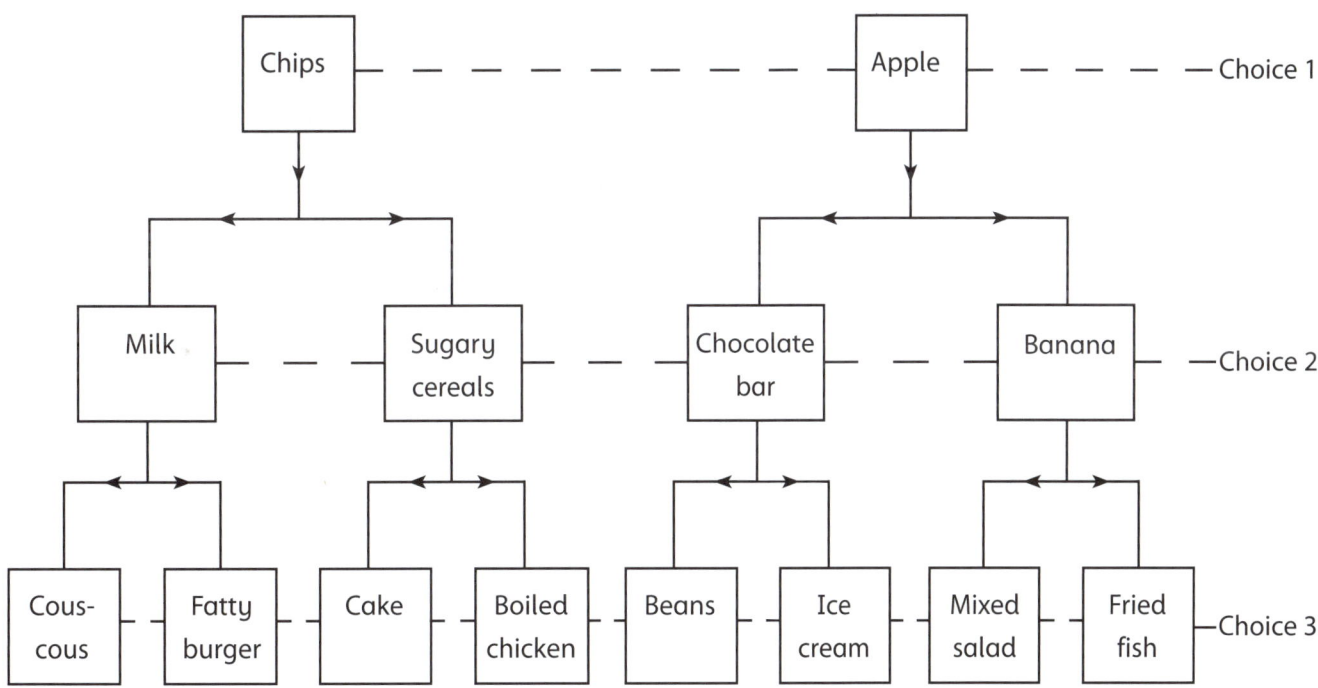

② Growing Plants

3 a Look at the parts of the plant and label them. Use the words from the word box.

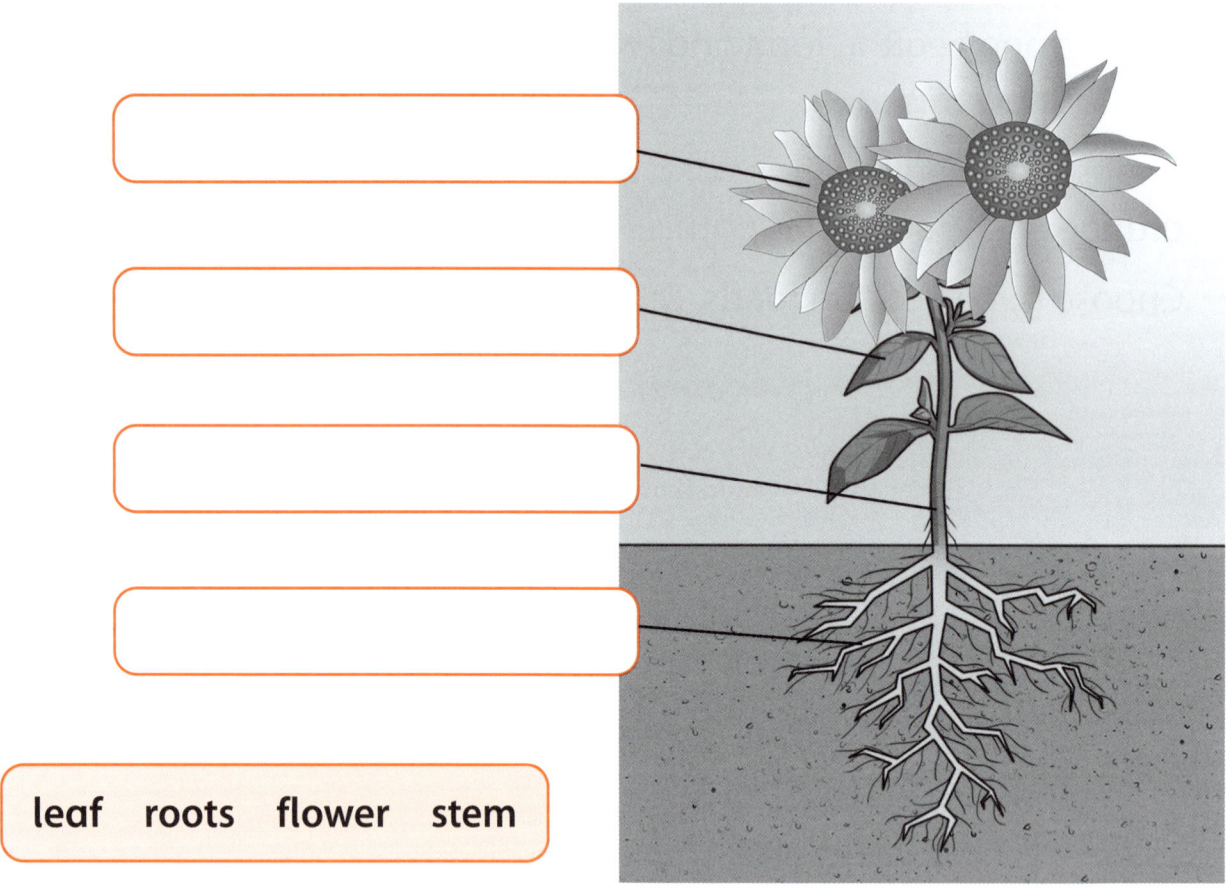

leaf   roots   flower   stem

b We can eat some parts of plants. Which parts of a plant do these foods come from?

Write:

- l for leaves
- s for stem
- f for fruit
- r for roots.

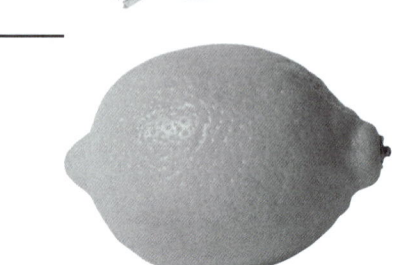

_____

_____

4 Three seedlings are planted in pots.

Pot A has soil that has been watered.

Pot B has sand that has been watered.

Pot C has soil that has not been watered.

Draw pictures to show what each of the seedlings will look like after one week. Colour in your pictures.

Pot A

Pot B

Continued overpage

Pot C

3 Habitats and Food Chains

5 Look at the pictures of animals. Are they birds, fish or mammals? Draw a line from each animal to the correct circle.

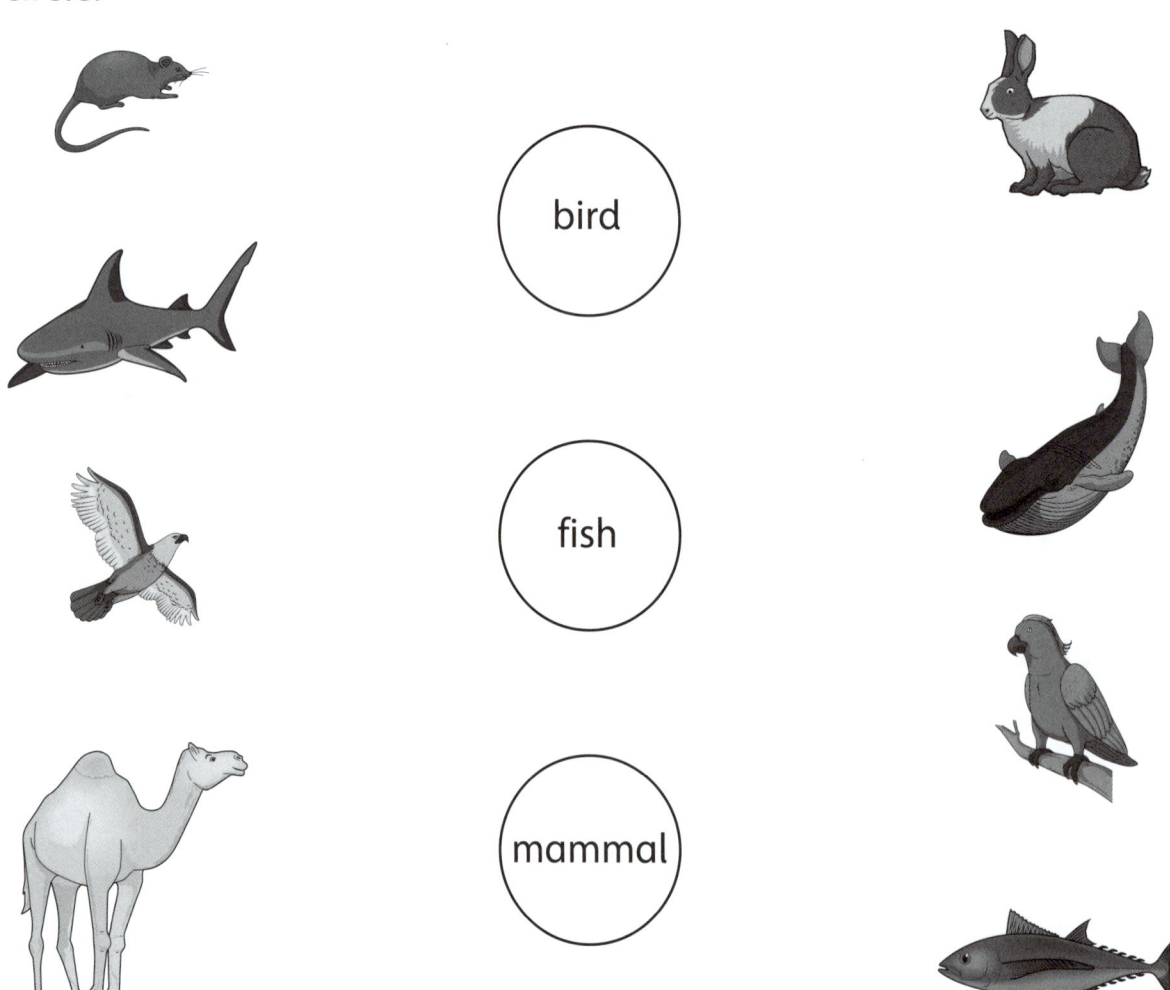

bird

fish

mammal

6 Tick ✓ the pictures that show living things.

4 Uses of Materials

7 Follow the curly lines to match each material to one of its uses.

Write one property of each material in the box.

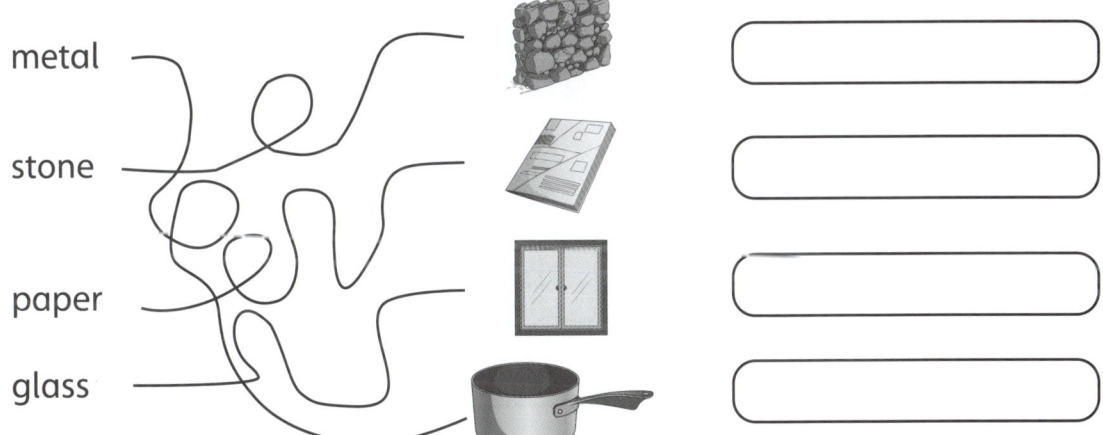

8 Tick ✓ the material that is the most absorbent.

paper towel ☐   cloth ☐   plastic bag ☐

9 Find the missing jigsaw pieces to complete the sentences.

Elastic	bands	will	_____
Metals are hard	and useful	for	_____
Bridges cannot be	made from paper	because they would	_____

saucepans.   break.   stretch.

10 Draw a line from each action word to the correct picture.

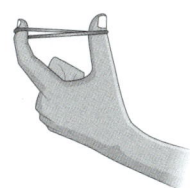

squashing

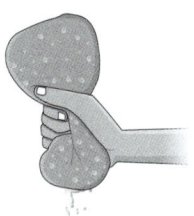

stretching

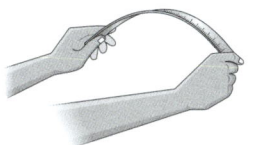

twisting

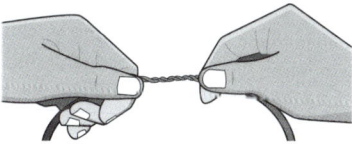

bending

11 Match each object with how much it has stretched the spring.

Draw a line between each spring and the correct object.

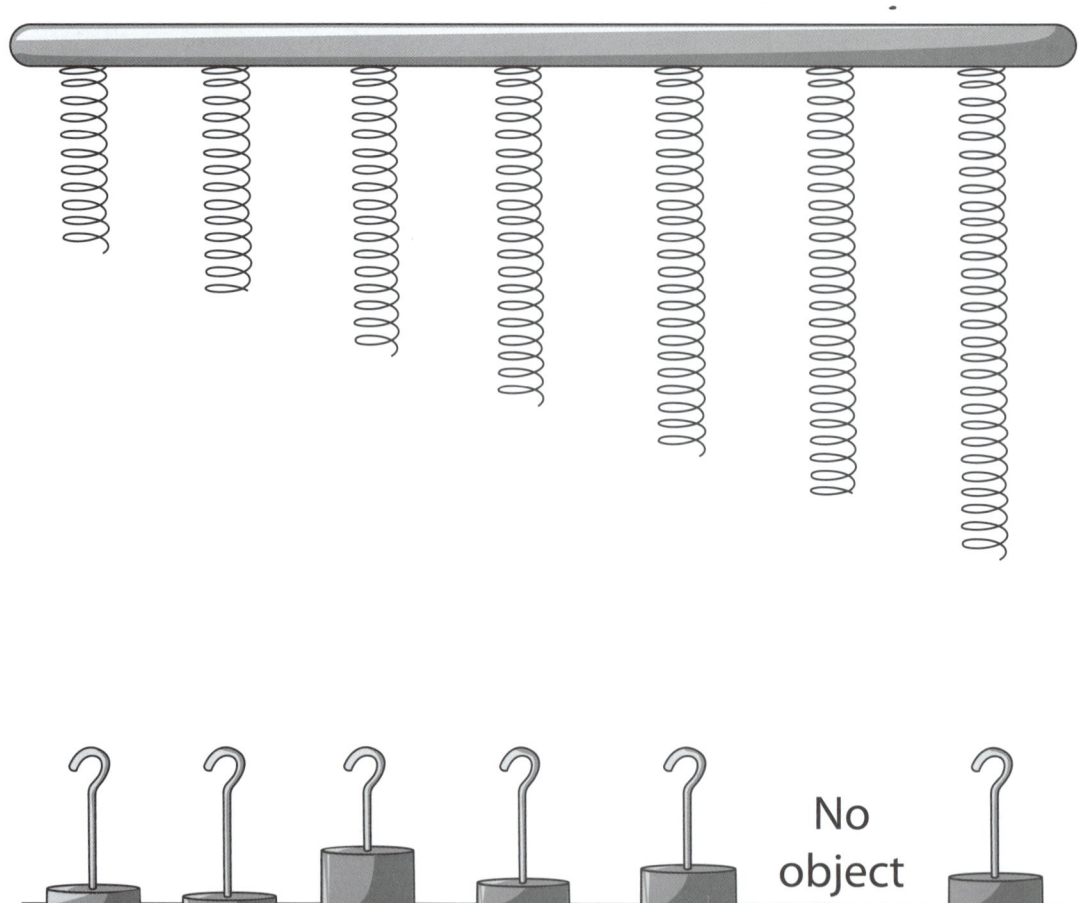

No object

⑤ Day and Night

12 a Look at the positions of the Sun in the sky.

Write the letter for the correct time of day on each Sun to match its position.

Choose from the words below.

a afternoon   **b** sunrise   **c** evening

d midday   **e** morning   **f** sunset

b Tick ✓ the correct answer.

The Sun moves across the sky. ☐

The Sun appears to move because the Earth is spinning. ☐

east   west

13 When would you see each of these shadows?

Label each picture with the correct time of day.

east   west

○──────────────────────○

east   west

○──────────────────────○

14 a Complete the missing word.

The path of the Moon around the Earth is called its o _ _ _ _ .

b Draw a full Moon, a waxing crescent Moon and a new Moon in the boxes below. Write the name of the phase of the Moon under each box.